Sweet
Aum

So love you

MW01075208

Own Your Life

How Our Wounds Become Our Gifts

Lise Porter

Copyright © 2017 Lise Porter

All rights reserved.

ISBN: 0-692-86185-8
ISBN-13: 978-0-692-86185-1

DEDICATION

To Chuck and Cindy Hoffman, Lynn and Vernon
Schwartz, Barbara Dixson, Rosy O'Bryant,
and Cathie Wegrzyn

CONTENTS

ACKNOWLEDGMENTS

I've wanted to write a book from the time my mother first put one in my hands. What I didn't realize is that just when you think you've written something brilliant, you discover it's awful or needs serious revisions. So as with knitting, you rip out stitches and try again. And again and again.

It can take considerable time to figure out a book's core message, its target audience, and its packaging. Writing this book has been a process that allowed me to synthesize my thoughts about healing while also reaching out to others. I am grateful to the individuals who read numerous early drafts and provided encouragement. Thank you, Tremper Longman, Hal Zina Bennett, David Read Johnson, Blair Glaser, Carrie Hill, Jill Corey Kluesner, Daniel Kirk, Peter Enns, Todd Johnson, Michael Spatuzzi, and James Radack. I express gratitude for Cait Levin's copy edit and Kate Murray's final edit. Thank you to Matt Dean for design expertise, Julia Verdin for PR advice, and Amy Beam for design and marketing strategies. And last but certainly not least, thank you to my blog and Facebook readers. You helped me find my voice and provided invaluable support.

Introduction

Our Wounds as Gifts

In California, we celebrate the Day of the Dead. I always think of my mom at this time of year. She loved Halloween, which happens to coincide with El Dia de los Muertos. In October, tombstones dot the yards in neighborhoods and cobwebs hang from trees.

I smile as I reflect upon this time as a child. My mother would take me to the school carnival and afterwards trick-or-treating with one of my friends. Even in my adult years, my mom always sent See's candy with a ghost or Jack O'Lantern card.

Now when I see candy appear in the drug stores, often as early as August, a lump forms in my throat, for I will never receive a box of candy from her again. Her sister, Kathy now writes me holiday notes. Sometimes when I pull one of Kathy's cards out of the mailbox, I think it's from my mom because their penmanship has similarities. Then I remember that my mom is dead and that her last letter to me was a suicide note-and I shake my head, trying to orientate myself. Is it possible she is really gone?

My mother took her life after release from prison for her fifth felony DUI. She had attempted suicide twelve years prior: she'd jumped from her apartment balcony, breaking a few ribs and puncturing a lung. She had just finished serving her first incarceration. She survived that attempt, but eventually shame and humiliation claimed her.

Like my mom, and like me, we all have a story. Never assume that because someone isn't sharing his or hers, there isn't one. We often make judgments and assumptions about other people, imagining that their lives have been easy because they seem to be doing so well and never seem to struggle with anything. But the reality is, if you are living in a human body, you have certainly encountered some degree of loss or at least a few challenges. This is a part of life for all of us.

Even those of us who haven't experienced an intense trauma possess some degree of wounding, because we are all impacted by the disappointments we face in life. When we swim in the ocean we have to learn how to handle the currents and the waves. I believe this is true for healing as well: it is about contending with problems, not just waving a magic wand and miraculously making difficult things disappear.

As a psychotherapist and national educator on mental health issues, I am consistently surprised by how much we can suffer. Yet I am equally moved by how we all endure and thrive. As individuals, people are remarkably resilient. *Own Your Life: How Our Wounds Become Our Gifts* explores how we move from crisis, challenge, or loss to a place of thriving in our lives.

When I was studying psychology a classmate asked, "When do people's issues finally resolve?" The teacher responded, "You never want to get rid of your wound. Your wound is your gift." Yet how we transform difficult experiences into valuable commodities is a whole different story – one requiring grit, creativity, and hope.

Just as we take steps to maintain our physical health, we can take steps to maintain our emotional well-being. *Own Your Life* provides insights and strategies for this. When I sat down to write this book, I wondered if we really needed another self-help/psychology book on the market. But gauging from my experiences teaching people all over the country, the answer is yes. Many individuals want resources because they are in emotional pain- and although there is literature already available that addresses this issue, folks are starving for narratives that provide hope when it comes to healing. These chapters are a collection of my thoughts and experiences related to this transformation and how we can own our lives. I invite you, the reader, to consider your own evolution as we embark on this journey together.

Chapter 1

Diamonds in the Rubble

I once heard a talk that compared our understanding of suffering to viewing a medieval tapestry. If you look at the backside of a tapestry, all you see are knots and tangled threads. If you look at the other side however, you see a magnificent pastoral portrait.

It is a very human tendency, though, to question why loss occurs and to try to make sense of it, even when it seems impossible to extrapolate any type of meaning. In the process, we typically blame ourselves, God, or something (or someone) else for what has happened. I was once talking with someone who had Parkinson's, for example, and she said, "I don't understand. I always did everything right. Who imagines that they're going to get a horrible debilitating disease? It has to be somebody's fault."

How nice it would be if all we had to do was dot our "i's" and cross our "t's" to be immune from hardship. Instead, hardship can hit us like a tsunami, lifting us out of the blue and dashing us against the rocks. I remember going to one of my mother's court hearings for a felony DUI. The proceedings took all of five minutes. The district attorney- a sour-faced, middle-aged woman- called my mother a "menace to society" and looked at her like she was a cockroach. Then the judge gave his ruling, sentencing her to two years in state prison. The next thing I knew, the bailiff was handcuffing my mom and whisking her away. As he escorted her out, I willed my mom to look at me, but she never glanced up.

I had to go to work afterwards. I recall feeling completely exhausted as I pulled into the parking lot of the hospital where I was employed. I took a deep breath, pulled out my ID badge, and walked inside. After the dinner break, I walked into the locked ICU, the most acute of the psychiatric units. I chatted with patients for a few minutes to get a feel for who was there, then walked back to my office. I was in no mood for facilitating a psychotherapy group, so I picked up a pack of UNO cards that were on a shelf and took them to the unit, along with some art supplies and a boom box. Of course the patients were delighted with the change of the game plan. No process group tonight. I sat and played cards with the patients- individuals hospitalized for psychosis, suicide attempts, and detox- and at some point, I felt a stillness descend upon the room. While we were engaged in the mundane activities of playing cards and listening to music, a sense of meaning had entered the room.

When I arrived home that evening there was a package on my doorstep. I looked at the return address and saw that it was from a good friend of mine, Debbie. She had been crocheting me an afghan, and I realized this must be the finished product. As I pulled the soft, pale-colored wool from the box, I held it to my cheek. She had sent a security blanket to comfort me. And with that, I found meaning in the absurdity that had been my day.

It is never our place to tell someone there is meaning in a tragic situation. Who are we to tell an individual that being raped is for a higher good or that our loved ones are in a better place if they have passed away? When terrible things happen, life is at its most incomprehensible and miserable. I'm not sure there is any true meaning in loss, violence, and tragedy. What I am interested in, though, is how humans find beauty even in the darkest of circumstances, and how we often create something new from ruin.

Meaning through Creation

When I think about the afghan Debbie crocheted for me, I think about the tremendous power creativity has to help us transform our lives. Creativity assists us by allowing us to organize the chaos of our lives- and to make something of beauty from it. For instance, when I was little, I was enamored by the fact that my grandmother knit. I'd watch her needles clicking and her fingers looping yarn around them, and marvel as a sweater began to take shape. The ultimate thrill was how something could be made from nothing-or at least from a string of yarn.

For something to emerge from a void or chaos is indeed a miracle. And for those of us who feel our lives have been shattered or whittled down to a thread, creativity becomes a force that can breathe new life and possibilities into us. Through this healing agent, we can break through stagnant situations and transcend them. As Albert Einstein once said, "Logic will take me from A to B- imagination will take me anywhere."

Creativity is a trait inherent to all human beings. It is not something doled out to the elite or those born with special talents. Every single one of us has the seeds of creativity within us. It is an aspect of how we are made in the image of God, for no other creature but humans and God can create. While all animals and even vegetation can procreate, only humanity can conceptualize something and bring it into existence. We are the only ones who can transform the idea of a building into the splendor of a cathedral, or take an emotion and translate it into a painting.

When there is enough heat and pressure, carbon atoms transform into the stones we know as diamonds. While I would not wish hardship on anyone, and while I don't know if we can say there is certain meaning in loss and catastrophe, I do find it interesting how nature often creates magnificence under adverse conditions.

Given the healing properties of the creative act, perhaps it is not unusual that creation itself reflects this process too. Who would have imagined that land erosion over millions of years would result in something as stunning as the Grand Canyon? Perhaps, then, we find meaning not so much in loss but in the moments of surprise and beauty that occur despite the dark times in our lives.

CHAPTER 2

Inviting Love into the Places Where We Hurt

After all the years I've spent doing healing work, I'm convinced the most fundamental tool for transforming wounds is love. And I'm not necessarily talking about romantic love. While the stuff of fairy tales and Hollywood- two people finding each other and sailing off into the sunset- is lovely, I'm talking about love in a more universal context. I'm talking about loving one's neighbor and learning to love oneself.

They say we learn about love through being loved by others. They also say we have to love ourselves before we can love another. But what if it is less formulaic than that, and far more magical? What if it is a little bit of a mystery? What if it is a mix of being loved *and* of learning to love oneself? What if we can keep learning about love as we grow, even if we have come to think that love is only for the lucky?

When I think of love, an image of a cat or dog rubbing up against someone's leg comes to mind. Did someone teach the animal to do that? Or is this impulse for contact left over from their days of being raised in a litter? Could it be natural curiosity that brings these animals toward humans? And what makes us respond in turn?

I don't know the answers to these questions. I only know what happens when we close our hearts and try to keep love out. The cost of not opening to love is akin to death. Love is what keeps us alive. It's the power that resonates through the universe. Without it, we shrink and become less human. Babies die if they aren't held, and adults fail to thrive when their hearts grow bitter.

It's not uncommon, though, to become protective of our hearts as we age. If we've been hurt badly, we don't want to make ourselves vulnerable. Allowing love to flow requires a degree of risk. Someone can shun our love or betray us. Someone may leave us or die. When any of the above happens, who wants to love again? Love can truly hurt. There is a reason we use phrases like a "broken heart" and "heartache" to describe how we feel when we've lost a loved one or a relationship ends.

This creates a terrible conundrum. We need love and we want love, but when we suffer from it we often decide we're not going to seek it out anymore.

Bringing Compassion to Our Pain

Sometimes when we are profoundly hurting, all we feel is alone. We want to act loving toward others, but if we feel broken and empty inside, sometimes it's hard to be kind and generous. How, then, do we break this cycle of emptiness and pain?

When a child skins her knee, if she is lucky and well cared for, an adult will swoop in and give her a hug- and soon the boo-boo starts to feel better. As adults, however, we often don't have this benevolent parent figure or kind angel at our side ready to comfort and reassure us (and perhaps we never did even in our youth). This is where the Herculean task comes in. This is when life demands that we learn to love ourselves.

As hard as it can be, we have to imagine that we are our own Fairy Godmother. When we stumble and fall, when life pushes us down and we sit on the playground crying, we have to come to our own side, soothe ourselves, and deliver the pep talk.

This is far from easy to do. It's much nicer when we have a loving person at our side protecting and nurturing us. But sometimes we simply don't have that support. So, as if we are doing calisthenics religiously, we must acknowledge that we need and deserve love and vow that we will show up for ourselves every day. We must affirm that we will be kind to ourselves in simple, basic ways, such as getting enough sleep, eating well, and allowing time for exercise and leisure. And we must also show up for ourselves by limiting the negative chatter in our brains that insists we are stupid, unlovable, or not good enough. We must imagine that we are no different from anyone else. If we wouldn't be unkind to others, we must not be unkind to ourselves. The more we care for ourselves, the more we start to fill up with a sense of peace. This in turn allows us to interact in the world with softer, less resentful hearts.

When Love Surprises Us

One of the ways we are transformed by love is when it simply surprises us. Herein is that sense of mystery. In the same way that winter eventually melts into spring, sometimes a period of isolation, loneliness, and bitterness suddenly transforms because of a variety of factors. Perhaps we're simply bored with our own hardened hearts and know that something has to give. Or perhaps someone or something in the environment touches us, reconnecting us with our sense of humanity.

It seems that one of the ways in which love starts to flow into our places of hurt is when we allow a little give and take between ourselves and others. For instance, in my early years of being a therapist, I worked on a children's unit in a psychiatric hospital. Many of the children had been victims of sexual assault, abandonment, and neglect. Shortly after that internship ended, I worked in a children's residential center- a place where kids were sent to live after being separated from their biological families.

At the residential center, staff and residents ate in a common lunchroom. On my first day there, as I was carrying my lunch tray to a table, I suddenly felt arms latch on to me from behind, gripping me in a fierce bear hug. I was so startled I almost dropped my tray of food. When I was able to disengage and see who was hugging me, I recognized a young girl whom I had treated at the psychiatric hospital. And I could see in her eyes that I meant more to her than I had ever realized. I'd spent maybe a total of four clinical hours with her, and yet somehow, I was significant to her.

I realized then that we never fully know the difference we're making in someone's life. This young girl was probably surprised at being cared for by the hospital staff and I, the young intern, was equally surprised to feel love coming back to me from the heart of my patient.

This exchange of energy is important to cultivate. We must learn to reach out to others, and we must learn to be receptive when others are giving to us. When we do, love then almost becomes like the exchange of oxygen- a constant cycle of inhalation and exhalation. This is how our wounds transform. Even when we feel our hearts have been bludgeoned, kisses of care can heal them.

Once, years ago, I had an experience in which I was so overcome by grief that I broke down weeping on a toilet in an airport restroom. As I came out of the bathroom stall, I glanced in the mirror. I looked like a drowned rat with puffy eyes. All my beauty and vitality had washed away, just like the mascara running down my face.

I thought I was alone in that moment- but I wasn't. A young woman approached me and asked, "Do you need a hug?"- and even though I was embarrassed, I nodded yes. I'd learned that when someone offers kindness, I shouldn't refuse it.

The young woman put her arms around me and I started convulsing with sobs- the kind that make you sound like a dying animal. She simply stroked my back like I was her baby that needed soothing. She didn't flinch or pull away: she waited a full five minutes, until the wailing subsided. When it finally did, and I looked up, I saw that she was crying too.

They say that God cries when we cry. Perhaps that's true. Even though my heart still hurt, seeing that woman's tears, I felt so much less alone.

CHAPTER 3

Birth Pangs

When the birthing process starts, blood-tinged discharge flows from the cervix. Later, water and other fluids gush forth. Then, during active birth, the labor is long, with intense pain, pushing, and contractions. After birth, there are all kinds of physical side effects, including sore breasts, constipation, tearing, and hemorrhoids- and on top of all this, the mother may experience a range of negative emotions, including irritability, sadness, or crying, commonly referred to as the "baby blues" (or "postpartum depression," for the more technical among us). This is how we enter the world.

Birth is a form of transformation. We start as the union of an egg and sperm, develop from cells in the womb, and eventually grow large enough to push ourselves out into the world. It's a messy process, and when we leave the dark, warm uterus, the shock makes us wail loudly in dismay.

Birth is also a dangerous process. The mother can die and so can the child. To get through it requires enormous courage on the part of the mother. Even with a midwife, doctor, or loved one nearby, she experiences the pain and uncertainty of the process by herself. This is an apt metaphor for our rebirth. We might have help (and ideally should), yet the journey down the birth canal is ours alone. We are both mother and child, giving birth to something and being born in tandem.

I'm not certain why we suffer so when we give birth to new phases of our lives. I don't know why the heart so often must break in order to feel, or why our insides are torn apart at the time of crowning. It's helpful, though, to normalize this and to know that at the end of the process there is great joy that can eclipse the pain we just experienced.

Years ago, when I worked in a psychiatric hospital, patients would often refer to the fact that they were there because they'd had a "breakdown." They saw their hospitalization as something inherently bad. For many, stress had so consumed their lives that they could not take the pressures anymore. I always encouraged them to try to view their hospitalization not as a breakdown but as a break*through*. What could be born from the pain of their illness (if they had a diagnosis), or from the emotional overload that had landed them in the hospital? How could they discover a new way of taking care of themselves after having a time of rest, reflection, and support?

I call this the gestation period. It takes nine months for the baby to develop inside the womb and eighteen years for a child to grow into an adult. Similarly, when we adults are going through our own kind of birthing we need time for development, nourishment, and plenty of rest. Without these elements, transformation is near impossible: instead we become like rats on a wheel, going in circles- going nowhere.

Yet who has time to rest in today's fast-paced society? No one. The only way to get that time is to give ourselves permission to take it. We are allowed to do that. We actually have a responsibility to do that.

It's okay to withdraw a little from the world. It can be healthy. Isolating and being less social doesn't necessarily mean we're depressed. And even if we are depressed, we may need that extra quiet time by ourselves to tend to the depression. We need people and activity too, of course, yet there is great value in pausing. It allows us to integrate our experiences.

I once saw a picture of a blue heron resting along a riverbed. I was temporarily arrested by the bird's beauty and the stillness of the water. The photo brought to mind a different pace- a time when summer was deeply intertwined with a slower rhythm. It reminded me of my childhood, when summer was a stretch of months where I occasionally felt bored and adults sat on their porches in the evenings with a glass of lemonade or a gin and tonic.

Although a challenge, it's possible to cultivate a bit of stillness within the demands of contemporary life. It might be that we spend a weekend reading a novel instead of running endless errands. Maybe we get take-out food or eat peanut butter out of a jar, if we don't want to hassle with the grocery store. Perhaps we exercise more or spend time in nature to break the pattern of our racing, never-ending thoughts. Then again, we might simply look at a photo of nature and for a few seconds stare into the greater expanse of existence, a place where we can be still.

In nature, the butterfly's transition from cocoon to winged creature is a wonder. It is also a glaring reminder that profound change requires stages of withdrawal and contraction. Yet nothing in our society supports this truth. We're supposed to get over pain quickly, immerse ourselves in external activities, and fake it 'til we make it. This completely contradicts the natural evolution process.

Butterflies are classic symbols of transformation. They start as eggs, transition to caterpillars, and then morph into cocoons. From that chrysalis state, they eventually emerge as butterflies. But it is not an easy metamorphosis. To the outside eye, the cocoons look ugly. They look like nothing. They look dead. All color and life force drains temporarily from them. Furthermore, the caterpillar goes it alone. She does not take a lover into the cocoon or host a dinner party in it.

For all of us, as the caterpillar, it's an arduous process breaking out of that lonely shell- but when we do burst out of the cocoon, we are no longer the same. We become a whole new being that can fly and dazzle the world with the bright colors of our wings. Ultimately, transformation beautifies us and frees us.

CHAPTER 4

For Some, For Others, For You

I have a colleague who often talks about a traumatic car accident she had when she was sixteen. Hit by a drunk driver, she almost died. It took months for her physical injuries to heal, and significantly longer for her psychological scars to heal. She was afraid to drive and became increasingly isolated. Distraught, she asked her mother, "When will I be normal again?" Her mother looked at her and quietly said, "For some, for others, for you."

My colleague's mother was basically saying that normal might as well be a setting on a dryer. Each person's life and experience are so highly unique there is no such thing as normal. There is only what is true for the individual.

What a beautiful way to conceptualize healing and recovery. There is no cookie-cutter formula for getting better, and there is no specific timetable, either. The best thing we can do when coping with adversity is approach our process with curiosity and compassion rather than judgment. Instead of asking, *Why am I not over this yet?!*, we can instead ask, *What is still hurting that needs love and attention? What do I have yet to learn from this irritation and sting? How can I soothe the pain and transform it into something of beauty that affirms my life instead of negating it? And how can I help myself, and in the process help others?*

My friend's story reminds me of the emotions we experience during challenging times, for they require a similar strategy of observance and patience. Paying attention to our feelings and understanding the role they play is critical.

Even animals express emotion. I once heard a story about a baby orca that had been separated from his mother. He was out in the ocean crying for her. Fishermen heard the high-pitched wails. Orcas stay close to their mothers throughout their entire lives, so the baby was quite distressed. To help him, the men rode alongside him, until he found a pod of other whales to join.

We have this same emotional wiring, but unlike animals, we learn early in life to monitor and repress our feelings. Holding back our emotions helps us fit into society and function when we have a job to do. It is common to compartmentalize our emotions temporarily. But there is a long-term cost: our feelings can become blocked in our bodies, causing a host of problems, including physical illness. Can you imagine that baby whale not allowing himself to cry for his mother? I certainly can't- yet we do the equivalent when we suppress our own pain.

While feelings may be intense at times they inform us about what is happening in our lives. They are mechanisms that help us respond to various situations. Emotions simply provide us raw data. Our work is to learn how to interpret that information.

The Risk Of Expressing Emotions

Expressing feelings can be scary, particularly if they have been bottled up for a long time. It can feel like losing control. Yet when we deny our feelings, we actually stand more of a chance of losing control than we do when we express them. Suppressed emotions can leak out in subconscious ways. We might suddenly snap at a loved one or drive too aggressively on the freeway because of the built-up tension we're trying to ignore. It doesn't have to be this way, though. The more conscious we are of what we're feeling and how to work with these feelings, the more choices we actually have. We can learn how to respond to difficult feelings in constructive ways.

When we realize that expressing emotions simply releases energy, we feel much more at peace about letting that energy flow through us. It doesn't have to control or consume us. We can remember that our feelings are a *part* of us, not *all* of us.

The idea that expressing emotions is a sign of weakness stems from cultural biases and stereotypes. Many of us were taught to suppress vulnerability as children. We might have been shamed or scolded for crying or expressing frustration or sadness. Perhaps we were told, "The world wants your smiles, not your tears," or even "Cowboy up and be strong." These messages reinforce stoicism- but the truth is, facing psychological pain actually requires the bravery of a soldier who walks straight into battle, chin held high. It takes guts. It also results in an authentic way of being in the world that allows us to be true to ourselves.

If we fell down and skinned our knee, people would think nothing of offering us a Band-Aid. Yet emotional wounds do not always elicit the same kind of attention. Sometimes people walk away. They can feel uncomfortable because our emotional expression forces them to acknowledge their own pain. Or they might want to comfort us but fear they will be intruding on our privacy. This is unfortunate, because in situations like these, comfort would be most ideal. Even if we like to be left alone when we are struggling emotionally, it's still nice when someone offers to be there with us. We can always say "no" if we would prefer solitude.

A friend once told me that when a bone breaks, the bone actually grows back stronger. True or not, our emotional wounds heal in a similar fashion. Pain can make us feel broken, yet as we heal, we often come back stronger than we were before.

Chapter 5

Breaking Up the Pity Party

While it's crucial to respect our process and honor its unique timetable, we also want to avoid the very real trap of self-pity. Not that I haven't been guilty of falling into this trap-in fact, if a prize were given out for most self-pity, I'd probably win. Over the years I've had to work hard to prevent my "woe-is-me" mantras from taking my mind straight into the gutter.

It's hard to listen to self-pity, whether it's our own mumbling or someone else's. While genuine expression of emotion increases intimacy and empathy, self-pity pushes people away. When I was a young girl, for example my mother would often tell me how miserable her life was because she was twice divorced. I hated it when she talked nonstop about this. I wanted her to be happy and to stop blaming her misfortunes on others.

When we find ourselves lacking empathy for people caught up in self-pity, it can help to remember that deep at its root is tremendous pain. At ten years old, I couldn't possibly fathom my mother's heartbreak. Two husbands had left her for other women despite the fact that she was a loving, attractive, and supportive spouse. This had broken her heart and shattered her self-esteem.

Often, we pity ourselves because something deeply sad and painful was never acknowledged. In feeling sorry for ourselves, we are trying to soothe and honor that hurt. Unfortunately, this method of trying to care for wounds typically backfires: because we get caught up in our narratives about all that is wrong and not working in our lives, we typically bypass the hard work of grieving that would allow us to eventually transform and release our heartaches.

If we self-pitiers finally stopped talking, we would probably break down sobbing. If my mom had done this, I believe I would have wrapped my arms around her because children understand raw emotions. It was her incessant complaining that I struggled to accept. I wanted her to take responsibility for her life and for her pain.

When The Airplane Circles But Fails To Land

If you've ever sat on an airplane that for some reason can't land right away, you know that the plane circles and circles for what feels like hours. The plane hovers over the landing strip until it can make its final descent- and when it does, it brings the passengers an enormous sense of relief.

When we are in the middle of self-pity, we are like that plane. Our thoughts circle and circle but never take us to a destination. We want relief and think that talking about our pain will bring it about, yet inevitably it doesn't. In order to feel peace, we need to fully express our feelings, and we also have to focus on what parts of our lives we have control over and make changes accordingly.

Our thoughts greatly influence how we feel about ourselves and about life. If we think that we are unlovable or that only bad things happen to us, we may be so clouded by these perspectives that we can't allow any new realities to emerge or coexist. This keeps us in a constant loop of self-pity and self-sabotage because the things we fear or that cause pain will keep recurring.

When I am really down emotionally, I try to get outside and to put myself in nature. Seeing flowers and hills and animals reminds me that there is beauty in the world and I am not alone. When I sense the strength of my own body and experience the sun and wind on my face and hair, I rejoice. I feel more connected to the life force that waves through the universe. Essentially, I try to get out of my head and to turn down the soundtrack that plays, "Woe is me, woe is me," over and over again. It's not that my life circumstances have changed or that I am any less solo in the world- but for a few minutes, I'm able to focus on how I am in partnership with life and how wonderful the world really is.

Self-Pity's Cousin

If self-pity had a cousin, its name would be "lack of personal responsibility." In addition to the deep pain that is associated with self-pity (underneath the kvetching), there is often a great fear or inability to take control of one's life. If we constantly complain about our circumstances, we end up with no time, energy or focus for creating a magnificent life. But it takes tremendous courage to own one's life. It's much easier to blame the world for our woes. The problem with this approach is, while it's true that life can be cruel, unfair, and brutally painful, fixating on what has been done to us leaves us with little will or motivation to effect change. No transformation can occur without an authentic grieving process, but part of grieving entails action and creative movement towards the unknown.

The challenge here is that if we take active steps away from self-pity and toward empowerment, our demons will most likely come out to haunt us. Every false belief we have, about ourselves or the world, will come back IN STEREO to try and persuade us that we can't own our lives and create change for the better- and like a hero or heroine in a fairy tale, we will have to get out our swords and slay these dragons. The monsters aren't just in our heads, either. All the people around us who are on some level committed to us staying stuck, whether consciously or unconsciously, will feed us the same lies: "You can't do that. Most people fail at that. Who do you think you are?"

Owning our lives is hard work. We actually have to do something. Whether we're trying to change careers, start a business, get out in the dating world, fine-tune a skill, or break a habit, we have to invest in the process. Like children learning to walk, we stumble and fall, and even if we have skinned a knee in the process, we need to get back up and try again. We have to lace up our sneakers and hit the pavement whether it's raining or snowing. We have to invest in our goals, though there's no guarantee of success and certainly no guarantee of a supportive team cheering us along. It's much easier to sit on the couch, eat bonbons, and feel sorry for ourselves. When it comes to the places where we have been the most wounded, it's very scary to create a new reality.

But They Have Such A Better Life

Part of what feeds the pity party is comparing ourselves to others. Media has given us all the false impression that life is supposed to be fantastic and amazing all the time. It has also injected us with very specific images of what happiness looks like. Then, when our lives don't fit that template, we feel like failures or freaks (or perhaps both).

Facebook, Twitter, television, music videos, commercials, and movies give us the impression that everyone out there in the world is ridiculously rich, beautiful, loved, adored, and having THE MOST AMAZING SEX ON THE PLANET every day- in fact, *three times* a day! We don't see photos of people sitting in front of the television at night and not talking to each other, or status reports about cheating spouses, or updates about families that are $100,000 in debt. Images of war-torn countries, poverty, famine, and rape also don't clutter up our feed as much as selfies do. If they did, we might not feel as sorry for ourselves. We also might feel inclined to reach out more to others.

I often think about what it was like to live in a different time period- an era when people were not influenced by mass media and technology. Did pioneers ruminate out on the prairies about the lives they were not leading? Or were they focused on their actual lives and survival?

Focusing on other people is a gateway drug to self-pity. It also prevents us from taking full authority over our lives. I remember once seeing a picture of a bride-to-be on Facebook wearing a sash at her bachelorette party, as if she were a beauty pageant contestant. It was actually a lovely photograph, as she was being authentically celebrated by her friends around an event that was joyous, a cause for celebration and being in the spotlight. Yet I remember thinking, *Am I not special or beautiful because I've never been a bride-to-be? Who am I if no special parties are ever thrown for me?*

Even as I engaged in this thought process, I recognized my own self-pitying tone. And again, underneath the woe-is-me thoughts was a feeling of genuine sadness. Many women dream about marriage. We're indoctrinated to do so in our upbringing. There's also a good reason why men and women both rejoice at the news of engagements and pregnancies: love and family are a major part of life. Yet how does it serve me to focus on not having a sash? What if I instead concentrated on what makes me special as a person with or without the sash?

These kinds of deeply personal questions are germane to all of us because we must embrace our worth independent of external circumstances. We abandon the pity-party when we stop caring so much about what others think about us or how we measure up. True transformation occurs when we embrace our lives just as they are, with all of their imperfections. This keeps things in perspective and helps us move forward in the direction we most desire.

Chapter 6

Becoming One's Own Beloved

"You've got to love yourself if you want to be loved," is a phrase that has always perplexed me, because we learn about love from other human beings. It makes love sound like a class you have to pass before you can enter college or something. How is one to learn to love oneself other than by example and by being loved by others?

Life doesn't occur in a vacuum. People need people and humans respond astonishingly well to love. Like plants receiving water, we are fed by it. If this weren't the case, babies wouldn't bask in the love of their caretakers and we wouldn't pine so much for the acceptance of our friends and families. Yet herein lies a huge issue. People can hurt us, betray us, and let us down. These are the foremost ways humans become wounded and personal transformation demands that we learn

29

how to deal with interpersonal hurts. How do we love ourselves when others retract their love, harm us, or disappoint us?

During difficult times, we tend to heal more quickly and to invite others into our lives if we love ourselves. So it becomes a "Which came first, the chicken or the egg?" thing. Do we learn to love ourselves from others loving us or do we love ourselves and then receive love in return?

The longing for love is a most primal drive for humans. It is what songs and stories are written about, and what most often motivates us. When we receive love, we're like puppies on our backs getting our bellies rubbed. We soak in the bliss. The reward of love compels us and the loss of love can make us feel as if we're dying.

When there is no one around to hurt us, some of us can do quite well. If our self-esteem is somewhat intact, and our abilities to self-soothe have been cultivated, we may live a very happy existence. Yet humans live interdependently, so everyone around us impacts us.

When a baby is young, helpless, and crying, we don't say to that child, "Here are your diapers. Figure it out." Instead, we pick up the baby and care for him or her. With time, the baby becomes whole and independent and can figure things out for him or herself. But even as adults, we can have places inside where we feel young and helpless. Wherever we have holes in our being from not being loved well or enough, we are more vulnerable. Healing can occur when we have experiences with people who meet our needs and love us in more complete ways. When our needs are then met in places where they weren't previously, we have a new perception of being. At some point though, we have to learn to love ourselves the same as we would love that infant: only then can our needs be met no matter who is or isn't there.

As with parenting a real infant, taking care of the small, fragile parts within us can be an exhausting process- and, at times, a thankless job. No one gives us a gold star for a task well done. Instead, we often do the work alone or with little help. We are indeed a single parent. While this might seem unfair, it is the only way to become one's own beloved because although other humans can delight us, they are also sure to sometimes disappoint us.

We live in a world that glorifies the flashy sides of love. Magazine spreads show couples holding hands, men on their knees proffering golden rings, and people so entwined they're practically copulating. I will be frank: The heart of self-love is not flashy, glamorous, or romantic. When we are learning to love ourselves, we don't get wined and dined. Self-love isn't delivered to us in a formula, or an orgasm, or a package from someone else. It doesn't come from buying a new dress or coloring one's hair. Instead it comes with the courage to face the pain of being human while still longing to keep our hearts open. What we really long for is a state of unity, which is only truly experienced with God. Whatever our religious beliefs, all humans want to feel bliss, wholeness, and peace. I believe we experience more of that when we feel at one with the desperate parts of ourselves.

Therapists are classically known for saying, "Just love yourself." But how do we actually do that? I am a therapist, so I've thought long and hard about this process and how to help others (and myself) with it.

For a long time I thought loving ourselves meant we looked in the mirror and liked what we saw. Or it meant that we cared enough about our bodies to exercise, eat right, and get enough sleep. What I've discovered is that while it's true that these are aspects of self-love, there are many more facets to it.

Small acts of self-love are actually huge. We learn to love ourselves when we experience hard-won victories, no matter how minute. Self-love comes when we take one step at the beginning of an incredibly difficult journey. Self-love comes when we choose not to reject ourselves, even if we feel as if we're standing by and watching the rest of the world cavort without us. Self-love comes when we stop looking in the window of that party and instead make our own, even if we're the only guest.

Acts of self-love occur when we focus on ourselves instead of on others. Acts of self-love occur when we choose forgiveness instead of bitterness, envy, or hate. Acts of self-love come when for every negative thought we have we realize we're only hurting ourselves. Acts of self-love come when we embrace every painful moment without numbing any aspects of it. Acts of self-love happen when we say, "I deserve more," or when we say to someone else, "Ouch. That hurt. Don't do it again!" And mean it.

When thinking about union with parts of the self, I sometimes reflect on the musical the *Phantom of the Opera.* Taken at face value, it is a haunting and dark love story. But it can also be viewed as a story of self-union: from a psychological perspective, the Phantom can be seen as representing a vital part of Christine, the heroine. It's not just a gothic tale with plush costumes: it's a tale of cosmic beauty.

What would it be like if the very part of us that we despise- that part that lives in the bowels of a church, like the Phantom- was also the part of ourselves that could serve as our angel of music, as the Phantom does? What if the deformed part of us, hiding beneath a mask, was the part most capable of inspiring creativity, beauty, and passion? Would it be possible to love this Phantom? Or would we run from him in fear?

The reality is that if we deny this part of ourselves, it will possess us. It will keep us captive, just as the Phantom did

Christine. Denial will haunt our dreams and wake us up at night. It will keep us prisoner from the light of day and make us forever victims. It will also bar those waiting to fully love us in a way we never imagined possible. It is only once Christine accepts the Phantom that she is able to love her true mate, Raoul.

Perhaps meeting our Phantom side represents the greatest love story ever. Here is the epic tale of befriending our own darkness and delivering him a kiss- of touching the deformed face under the mask with profound gentleness and compassion. And when we do that, perhaps we are finally liberated free to leave the basement of the church and free to stand in majesty, finally whole. Perhaps the world's greatest lover is right here inside us- embedded in the music of the night.

Chapter 7

The Beauty of Desire

The other day a dear friend was showing me the upstairs rooms in her new home. As we discussed her plans for decorating the guest room we both noticed the stuffed animals on the closet floor. The room had initially been intended as a nursery. It took only a thirty-second glance at those furry friends for me to feel the pain of her infertility. We moved on to view her husband's music room.

I wonder how many of us have put away the toys of our beloved dreams or have not even begun collecting them. My friend's dilemma reflects the very reasons why we sometimes won't allow ourselves to hope. Is it wise to keep wishing for something when reality informs us that this may never be a possibility? When waiting for our dreams to materialize turns into futility? At this stage what is the point of desire?

I have always been in awe of the heart's capacity to experience a constellation of feelings. In life we are plunged into a vortex of energy as mysterious and vast as the inside of a flower. Frequently, when we've had great loss or experienced intense pressures, we reflect more on the sadness and disappointment associated with life than the pleasure, joy and fulfillment it also offers. When this occurs, we are at risk of killing desire in all its forms, our zest for life seeping out of us like air slowly escaping from a balloon.

It is a stark reality of life that we don't always get what we want. Our dreams can and do get bashed. But somehow we must keep hope afloat in one way, shape, or form, even as we're coming to terms with acceptance, and this can be a tremendous challenge.

I have no simple answers for how to keep hope alive other than fanning the flame of desire, even if this means letting one dream die and opening to a new one. This allows us to "dwell in possibility," as Emily Dickinson once wrote- and somehow, hope creeps in regardless. I once heard hope referred to as a beach ball that we sit on and try to keep submerged under water, yet it keeps popping out from under us.

In religious circles, desire often gets a bad rap. Thought to lure one into avarice or lust, it is often represented as the devil incarnate or that wanton woman leading a man astray. In

Buddhism, desire is thought to be the root of all suffering, and thus craving is ideally eliminated. And yet transformation is impossible without desire. We need it for motivation.

Desire represents a primal evolutionary force propelling our species not just toward procreation but also toward learning, expansion, creativity, and growth. Ignited early in our lives, desire is how we learned to walk as children: Seeing an object, we longed to explore our world. As we turned our heads in the direction of our intrigue, we twisted our bodies and extended our arms in curiosity. Eventually, this stimulated us to crawl toward our mother or father, beloved toy, or family cat. Once we could stand and walk, we could go straight after what caught our eye with even more agility and speed.

Thus, desire is an impulse within us- one hopefully motivating us toward positive, pleasurable things. Children wake up early, desiring the day's start of play, (much to the chagrin of their parents). Dogs, too, register desire as they wag their tails in anticipation of a walk, the beach, or a bone. And as we humans age, we desire a range of things- the love of others, physical intimacy, material possessions, fruitful activities, and work well suited to us, to name just a few.

Through longing we have the energy to pursue our goals, and if our efforts result in joy, this reinforces our commitment. In its highest form, desire is a spiritual catalyst igniting our hearts to burn for something meaningful beyond ourselves.

But if desire plays such a significant role in transformation, why do we often fear it or feel numb instead?

The Ebb and Flow of Desire

When running psychotherapy and drama therapy groups, I often ask participants to make a wish for themselves at the end of the session. If one were to give this directive to a roomful of children, they would probably come up with ten wishes instead of one. And yet adults sometimes struggle to articulate even one wish for themselves. "What's the point of wishing? Nothing ever goes right in my life," people sometimes say. Other times people start to tear up at the thought of even expressing a longing or hope. What I've noticed is that when individuals have experienced a great deal of loss, the risk of desiring something brings a sense of sheer terror- and sometimes that terror turns to suppression of hope.

When you look at the ocean when it is calm, sometimes it takes a while for a wave to build- but slowly, that wave will gain momentum, and eventually swell, break, and crash to shore. Desire is similar. It crests and falls according to its own innate rhythms.

At the time that I first wrote this chapter, I had to unexpectedly put both of my beloved cats to sleep on the same day. One cat, Hafiz, had been ill with cancer, so his death I was prepared for (as best as one can be for such an event, anyway).

What I didn't expect was for his brother, Rumi, to become fatally ill twenty-four hours after I had made the decision regarding Hafiz. They were both fourteen years old and I had cared for them for seven years. They'd been more than pets to me; they'd been my family, my children and my beloved friends.

In the aftermath of their deaths and my subsequent grief, any sense of desire for a new pet feels dormant. My desire feels flattened out, almost nonexistent. And yet I know that at some point- not anytime soon, but eventually- the longing for a new pet will build in my heart again. When it reaches its apex, even if it's years from now, I'll enter the cycle all over again. But desire can't be pushed prematurely, and it can't be manipulated. It has to build in its own organic way, swelling with the tides at its own pace.

When we're in significant transformation cycles, it's important that we respect this rhythm. We do not expect flowers to bloom in winter; nor do we anticipate stagnation in summer or fall, at the height of nature's ripening and harvest. We lean into transformation when we understand this. In our current world, however, the messages we receive often contradict these natural patterns. We're always told to get back on the horse when we've fallen off, but perhaps both the horse and the rider need a little rest before attempting to gallop again.

Even as we take this time, though, it's important to watch the embers of desire as they slowly build back to fullness, for there can be such joy when we allow connection, pleasure, and fun in our lives. Despite the enormous grief we feel when something comes to a close, the experiences are worth having. As they say, it is better to have loved and lost than to have never loved at all.

When I speak of desire, I am not implying that life is one big hedonistic rush or that we can always feel good all of the time. Just as too much candy can make us sick, misdirected desire can cause tremendous heartache. But believing that we are worthy of happiness and that life is fundamentally good can change the course of our lives. Our heart's yearnings can serve as a GPS system when we're traveling down the road of transformation. Finding ways to fulfill these desires can help propel us through challenging times and shed light on our soul's deeper journey. When we experience even a modicum of joy, we begin to transcend the profound struggle inherent in existence- and the benefit of this is not merely self-serving. On the contrary, when we are tuned into desire and cultivate it in positive, constructive ways, we contribute to the world through our enthusiasm and joy, and we access our talents and passion for the benefit of others.

If we block our deeper desires, there will always be a part of us sleepwalking through life; we will never fully realize our dreams or potential. And this can be akin to death. Over time it can lead to depression, regrets, and a sense of futility, as if there is no longer any meaning in life. To use our wounds as gifts, we have to meet our fears of desire head on and somehow find the courage to sit in the unknown with our longings, even if it feels a little dangerous.

Chapter 8

Tolerating Pleasure and the Perils of Desire

Even when we understand the benefits of desire and its relationship to transformation, once we feel its presence in our midst, it can be hard to tolerate. Sometimes even pleasure, which brings such joy and ecstasy, is feared. We imagine its absence before we manage to settle into its presence, or we sense it might trigger some profound insatiability within us. We may also have some type of trauma associated with pleasure, which very much complicates our feelings. It doesn't matter what the gratification relates to: many of us are not comfortable with feeling good in some areas of our lives.

The reasons we struggle with pleasure are vast and varied and relate to the challenges of sustaining happiness. Can we live in an embodied state? Do we feel we are worthy of feeling good? Do we know how to sit with the discomfort we experience when emptiness comes after fulfillment? And what do we do with fears related to success or intimacy, or with guilt that others might not have as much as we do?

The pleasure that comes with attachments will always be fraught with tension, because as humans, we are in a constant state of connection and separation. The infant who loves being held in mom and dad's arms will cry when put down in the crib and separated from the bliss of human warmth and love. It is a profound sense of connection, or the possibility of it, that can suddenly induce a state of longing and aloneness that makes us want to crawl out of our skin. Somehow, though, we have to hold the paradox that we are simultaneously separate and in connection. Just because we have times of autonomy, doesn't mean that we are not still loved by or in union with the world around us. As we come to understand this and increase our tolerance for the inconstant state of pleasure, we can move more fluidly in the realms of transformation.

The Relationship Between Desire, Pleasure, and the Divine

Over the years I've come to realize that desire and pleasure more often than not reflect an impulse for connection with the Divine. If we were to strip down our raw impulses so they were free of the objects upon which they were directed, we would most likely discover a longing for spiritual unity. Whether we conceptualize this as a return to Eden or experience it as sexual ecstasy, I believe a longing to feel one with something else or to escape pain is what underlies desire. We all want to feel good, to experience wholeness and to give and receive love.

Perhaps, then, longing can best be clarified as a desire for one's most fully realized self to give and receive love. After all, what is it about the people, animals, and places we come to care about that induce such tenderness we sometimes can't even bear it? Why is a baby so soft and sweet you feel the presence of God when holding him or her, and why does a loyal cat or dog make you feel safe and secure? Perhaps we're all trying to awaken to the wonder that life is both within and around us. We are not broken; we simply long to awaken, and desire is part of that process.

It seems that the more we are in touch with this inherent need the more we can direct our desires toward a higher good. Through desire we can find the channels best suited for sharing the talents, lessons, and skills we've acquired over the course of our lives. Our gifts will be far better received if delivered in a package that we've enjoyed creating and that bears our own unique stamp of the Divine.

Transforming Misdirected Desire

To yearn is inescapable. It is the human heart screaming for nourishment. But to acknowledge desire, one must tolerate vulnerability: otherwise, our longings can become grossly misdirected. In fact, one of the impediments to seeking passion and pleasure in our lives is the fear that our desires will become misguided or out of control. And this concern is valid, particularly if our coping strategies in life have involved seeking pleasure or escape in random and destructive ways. We may have turned to drugs or alcohol, engaged in promiscuous relationships, or spent money beyond our means, only to discover that following these paths only created more problems and not transformation.

Our adult desires have to be channeled appropriately. We can't jump into bed with every man or woman we are attracted to any more than we can follow all the whims of our hearts. But what is the desire behind the impulse trying to communicate? When we feel attracted to a stranger or someone who is not our partner, is it because we are longing for intimacy? And when we feel that knee-jerk impulse to immediately quit our job and sail around the world, is it because we are longing for adventure or a different type of work? If we can stay with these desires, as uncomfortable and nerve-wracking as they can be, they may lead us to places in our development we never imagined or anticipated.

When I was a toddler, my parents told me on a family hike not to play too close to a stream in case I fell in- and of course I did, although I don't know whether this was an accident or happened through my own orchestration. I also drove my tricycle straight into the swimming pool on a different occasion. I was a small child, not fully aware of danger or the concept of defying my elders. I was, however, beginning to make choices- and one of those was playing in water at all costs.

My childlike fascination with water was not a bad thing in itself, and my parents understood that. They were smart enough to channel my attraction to water into swimming lessons and trips to the beach- and to make certain that no matter how much I loved being in the water, I listened to their commands. If I was to be allowed to swim, I had to follow their rules: otherwise, the privilege would be taken from me. In raising me this way, my parents taught me proper water safety, as well as exercise habits that I engage in to this day.

Now, as an adult, I swim almost every day, because it's one of the things in life that give me enormous pleasure. On days that I don't swim, I'm simply not as happy. And given how short life is, why not do something that brings pleasure?

Chapter 9

The Universe Supports Boldness

"He who hesitates is lost," my father used to say when teaching me how to drive. He was referring to passive drivers-people who hem and haw when changing lanes or merging onto the freeway, accelerating and decelerating erratically and never making their intentions known to other drivers. The result is comparable to having your foot on the gas and brake simultaneously. "People who drive too slow or without assertiveness are just as dangerous as those who drive too fast and reckless," my father asserted.

My father used to race stock cars as a hobby and was an excellent driver. I don't know that I can say the same about my skills, but I can say that his words stuck- and I've learned that they apply to many situations. A figure skater who goes into a jump at high speed and then pauses right before lift-off typically doesn't hit her mark and often lands on her fanny instead. Similarly, a surfer who hesitates when a wave fails to crest will not pop up correctly. He'll end up on his knees instead of standing up on the board. He also might miss the wave entirely, or take it at the wrong time, causing him to pearl and tumble into green water and foam. Being a surfer myself, I know these experiences all too well. They can be painful, embarrassing, and humbling!

The problem, of course, is that when we're going through significant change or have endured something quite challenging, we often feel hesitant. Bold is probably about the last thing we might feel. Perhaps our self-confidence has been beaten out of us, and we're frightened of uncertain outcomes. After all, bad things can happen. Yet so much about transcending difficulties requires boldness.

The real task, then, is recognizing the right moment and then committing to it. To jump on every wave does not reflect boldness- that shows foolishness or ignorance. The conditions need to be right: the wave needs to break with good form and without too many people on it. But when you are in the zone of a perfect wave, it is a Nike "Just do it!" moment. Do not turn away the gift horse.

"The universe supports boldness," a friend of mine said recently. This is such a quintessential California statement; it reads like a bumper sticker. And yet it is so spot-on. The universe most definitely supports boldness. No great achievement has ever come from being timid or from making a half-baked commitment. Greatness and transformation come from going all-in and risking both failure and success.

When I was eighteen, I was an exchange student in Bandung, Indonesia. For an entire year, I lived with an Indonesian family and went to an Indonesian school. Before I left America, people told me that I was brave to be going so far away. I remember thinking, *Huh?* At that age I didn't think about all the what-ifs or all the things that could go wrong. I only thought about the adventure: my eyes were focused on the excitement of travel and learning about a new culture. I think we adults have much to reclaim from the vivaciousness and boldness of youth.

It was a few years after my mom died that I first learned how to surf. This wasn't such an unusual sport to try, given that I was an avid swimmer, and I fell in love with it the first time I caught my first little wave on white foam using a Styrofoam board. After that, I went out every weekend to learn more about the waves and how to navigate them. I bought a wetsuit, rented a board, and then eventually bought my own board and surfboard racks to put on top of my car. It was the most adventuresome thing I'd done in ages!

I learned that the only way to surf was to be out there in the water no matter what. It was essential to suit up. Sometimes the conditions were poor: there would be little swell, and all of us would be out paddling around on our boards as if we were in a big bathtub or lake. Other times the sea would be fierce and angry– the waves too dangerous to even consider. Then I'd just wade around in the foam and watch like a child, standing along the shore. Regardless, I always enjoyed being out there in the water. I loved the healing properties of the salt and the sea and being around other people. It was like we were all kids at the playground.

Sometimes the currents just aren't ideal for catching a wave, but even so it is critical to be in the water. We have to at least paddle out to see what might happen. When we crash and tumble, we have to scramble back up on our board and try again. The ocean can be dangerous, but it is also glorious.

The friend who told me, "the universe supports boldness," was actually my co-lead in a short film that I wrote, produced, and starred in. Just before making the film, I'd gone through a terrible romantic breakup in which I had crashed and burned. To redeem myself from that year, I decided to finally put something in the can (as in, put something on film after years of dabbling in acting, writing, and cinema). I'd been too afraid to pursue an acting career after graduating from college, despite the fact that my major was in theatre. Then I'd been too afraid to move to Los Angeles, even though I continued to study acting for the next twenty years. But when I made this short film in Los Angeles with some filmmaker friends, suddenly I couldn't hold back anymore. At forty-six, I decided to pack up my life and move. It was terrifying, but within a month I'd landed a commercial that ended up airing nationally- and I never looked back after that.

When we are at our most broken, remember, "the universe supports boldness." So when we've fallen hard, why not try something outrageous? Sometimes we have nothing to lose and everything to gain.

Chapter 10

Be Here Now

To experience life fully and be attuned to our inner promptings, and needs, we need to be present- but in today's hectic world, stress and concern over just about everything under the sun can leave us feeling disembodied and checked out.

When my best friend had a baby, spending time with her child provided me with great practice at being in the here and now. Children and animals are generally great teachers on this subject, and I was lucky to have such a master. As my friend's son, Nils, got a little bigger each day, we slowly introduced him to different solid foods. One day, we put a few raspberries on his high chair tray for him to consume. As he crammed a raspberry into his mouth with his little fingers and he experienced the taste for the first time, he gave us a huge grin, as if to say, "Thanks, guys," and then started to clap his hands. For weeks, he clapped every time he ate a raspberry or a strawberry. When eating these fruits, his ecstasy was palpable.

This experience had a profound impact on me. Nils was born a month before my father was diagnosed with pancreatic cancer, which is a particularly aggressive form of the disease. Most people only live four months after being diagnosed, and my father was no exception: he died four months later.

While my father was dying, I spent a considerable amount of time with Nils and there was something especially profound about being with someone just entering the world when someone so important to me was about to leave it. Many times, being with Nils buffered the grief I felt after a visit to my dad at the hospital.

These were difficult times, and not just because he was dying. My father and I had actually been estranged for fourteen years when he was diagnosed with his cancer. My interactions with Nils were far less fraught than my interactions with my dad. Yet there were similarities between my visits with the two of them- namely, that both were rich and meaningful.

Nils and my dad had something in common during that time: because of their particular stations in life, they appeared more in touch with simply "being" than most of us are. Nils, having just come into the world, didn't have any notions about how to behave other than to just be. And my father, having experienced life, was no longer clinging to his ego for control. He was able to surrender his attachments to outcomes and also just be. Both Nils and my dad were living in the present.

Being in the moment opens us up to a variety of emotions, including joy. I noticed this when I was taking care of Nils. Whether observing his delight upon seeing a bird or a flower, or noting the smile on his face when I walked into his room to pick him up from his crib when he'd just woken up from a nap, Nils's exuberance moved me deeply. I was also struck by the pleasant rhythm of existence we fell into whenever I babysat for him. I'd arrive and we'd have breakfast. Then I'd sit on the couch and read while he sat on the floor and made new discoveries: how to grasp an object, how to roll over, how to make a sound. After about an hour of that, we'd get out the stroller and go for a walk. Then it would be about time for lunch. After lunch, he'd fall asleep in my arms as I rocked him to sleep. As he taught me how to focus on the here and now, my worries and struggles seemed to melt away.

Spending time with my father in the hospital had a similar quality, though it manifested in a very different way. Because my dad and I had been estranged, there was much I could have been angry with him about. But instead, the past often melted away when I sat next to him. We didn't talk about things, really. My dad didn't know how to say "I'm sorry," or how to speak intimately. But his eyes were warm and loving.

Underneath his personality and past negative behaviors, I saw a presence I had once loved and still did. As his body prepared for death, his spirit moved to the forefront of existence- making it possible for us to connect.

When my father passed, there was a surreal quality to his death, as if my life were going in slow motion and nothing really mattered except for being attuned to the experience. Although I continued to work part time, my job didn't matter so much. Household chores didn't, either. Everything got taken care of but without the habitual strain involved. It was as if time had stopped so that what was really important could be experienced and absorbed.

Challenges to Being in the Moment

Unlike Nils and my father just before his death, most of us struggle to stay present. While the concept of being in the moment might seem simple, in actuality it is quite difficult. In fact, one of the most predominant concerns I hear clients address in therapy is that it's hard for them to be truly aware or conscious. They often share that they feel like rats on a wheel, in perpetual motion with no reprieve. Many people work, raise children, and have endless social commitments, to the point where everything in life starts to feel either overscheduled or like something to simply be checked off of a to-do list. When this happens, it is hard to experience joy or to perceive meaning in our lives. Suddenly it is as if we have become a human "doing" instead of a human "being." Everything moves at a too-accelerated rate.

Multiple factors contribute to our stepping out of the present. One could make the argument, for instance, that the childlike freedom Nils experienced was bound to erode once he grew older and began to face responsibilities. And indeed, as we mature, more and more things can rob us of conscious presence. The challenge then is to live fully, regardless of the demands and stresses pulling on our energies.

In many ways, looking after Nils from time to time assisted me in the process of learning to live fully. While there is a routine to follow with a six-month-old child, an infant can't be micromanaged, nor can a child's day be exactly planned out. I knew Nils had a feeding and nap schedule but much of how the day unfolded required that I take my cues from him from moment to moment. If he cried, chances were his diaper needed changing, he was tired, or he was hungry. If he reached out his arms to me, chances were he wanted to be held. Each day for him seemed to unfold organically, and I needed to allow my life to do the same. My father was lying in his hospital bed with nurses and people looking after him. I could sit and worry nonstop about that, or I could pay attention to Nils and enjoy his beautiful smile and each new thing he learned. And when I was at the hospital, I could operate in the same manner, tending to my father from moment to moment and seeing to both his needs and mine.

Going from Moment to Moment

When being in the moment involves difficult emotions and we are taxed, it can be helpful to find ways to transition from one moment to the next so we don't drown in our own pain. While a small child can do this with a degree of alacrity, having a complete meltdown over dropping her ice cream on the floor one minute and then suddenly bouncing with happiness the next, by the time we are adults, we are not as adept at this process.

Part of the reason this happens is that over time, memories accumulate. We have an entire storage bank of circumstances that have resulted in emotional pain and thus we start to monitor ourselves to avoid re-experiencing situations that resemble previous hurtful ones. While in some ways this is good- we're learning from experience- our caution can also pull us out of the moment. We can become so hypervigilant and logical that we run the risk of never engaging fully and spontaneously. If we attempt to predetermine what is going to happen in our lives, we can miss opportunities for wonderful and surprising events to unfold.

Probably more than anything, paying attention to our breath can assist us in moving from one moment to the next.

Our bodies inhale oxygen and exhale the exchange twenty-four hours a day, regardless of what we are doing: when we pay attention to this process, however, we recognize our breath as a powerful current that transports us from one moment to another.

While in a yoga class I once heard sobs escape from a woman on the mat next me. My heart went out to her. Yet I also knew that as long as she kept breathing, the sobs would release and eventually abate. When we allow our breath to take us through pain, it's like a wave coming forward after the wave that preceded it has dissolved. A new moment arises.

Embracing the Moment

Playing with Nils when my father was so close to death brought me a very heightened awareness about my own mortality. When we're young we think we're going to live forever, but as we age we start to see that this isn't reality. For me, losing both of my parents was a huge wake-up call that it was important to make every moment matter.

Years ago, I worked as a nanny for three boys in Marin County, California, right across the Golden Gate Bridge. I had just graduated from college. My tasks included caring for the boys, cooking, and light housekeeping duties. One day the kids were just dying to show me something but I was caught up with dinner preparations. They approached me asking if I could come look at what it was they were doing. My knee jerk response was, "Not now." But then I looked into their eager faces, so full of excitement, and I checked myself. What was I doing that was so urgent? I followed them upstairs to see what they were up to and discovered that they had built a fort with pillows and blankets. As I complimented them on their work, their faces registered pride and joy.

In a society that puts great value on work and productivity, it can be easy to lose sight of what really matters. We wear our busy schedules like badges of honor and talk about not having time to eat lunch or spend time with loved ones as if it's something to boast about. But for those of us who have experienced great loss, part of the healing process is realizing that these things matter. A child looking up expectantly at us, an animal longing to be petted, or a flower begging to be admired are all things that can bring us great joy if we take the time to embrace what is right in front of us.

Chapter 11

Flying Blindfolded

One of the hardest things about going through tough times is that we never know how long we'll have to endure the situations and we can feel incredibly lost. It's almost as if we're flying blind, and that can be terrifying.

Pilots have to learn how to fly using their navigation instruments only. They do a period of training where they cannot rely on their eyesight- where they have to use other tools to keep on course.

When I think of navigation tools for our life journeys, the heart comes to mind. Throughout time, various civilizations have viewed the heart as the seat of wisdom. Given this, we would be wise to listen to what it has to say instead of ignoring it and always deeming its impulses as foolish. The heart is full of wisdom- it knows exactly where we are emotionally, what we want, and what would make us happy- and yet for some reason it gets a bad rap. In Western society especially, the heart is often viewed as inferior to the mind when it comes to processing information and making decisions.

So we are told to trust our minds, not our hearts, and are led to believe that the heart can get us into a lot of trouble. Perhaps this is true. But think of all the phrases we use on a daily basis: heart of the matter, heartache, change of heart, heavy heart, faint of heart, light heart, etc. If the heart so misleads us, why does so much of our vocabulary reflect its intelligence and ability to understand things?

I know that for myself the heart is a mysterious creature that I can't seem to get away from. Every time I want to leave it at home for the day, it follows me like a dog who won't leave my company. In fact, in many other ways it is like a dog: loyal, vulnerable, forgiving, fierce, and protective of those I love.

In therapy, when my clients are stuck in their heads and not making progress toward talking about what is really going on, I often ask, "If your heart could speak, what would it say? If it were sitting here right on the couch with you, what would it want to talk about? How old is your heart, and what does it want?"

Inevitably, this is when clients start to cry, because their hearts actually have a lot to say but have been ignored and censored for too long.

I'm not saying the heart is always right. We have to be wise when it comes to understanding its yearnings. But when we trace the topography of our hearts, we find ourselves in vast, wild, and beautiful terrain.

In Chinese medicine the heart is referred to as the Emperor because it reigns supreme. All the other organs are considered subservient to it. The liver is referred to as the General and is believed to be the organ in charge of making decisions. Once the liver makes a decision, the gall bladder then helps execute the order. It stimulates the energy required to put that activity into motion.

Despite the beauty of this system, we often fail to trust our instincts. We hear "You can't always listen to your heart" and "Go with your head, not your gut" all the time. I'm always perplexed when experts say we shouldn't make our decisions based on our emotional states. To divorce our emotions from the decision-making process negates the profound wisdom that wells up from our various body systems. Our bodies were designed to provide us with powerful information: they act similarly to a pilot's flight instruments. We can't afford to ignore that information.

When we fail to pay attention to our instincts, we often deeply regret it. In the Chinese system, this represents anarchy. This is when the body and mind go to war with one another.

It takes courage to follow decisions based on instinct. When we say, "He or she had the gall to do something," we mean courage is entailed. It takes supreme guts to follow the guidance coming from deep within our core.

We can only perceive information, though, if we're still enough to listen to our bodies' signals. If you've ever tried to have a meaningful conversation with a lot of noise or commotion in the backdrop, you probably found it difficult to concentrate. If there is too much interference, it is hard to hear. Turning down the volume on the stimuli around us helps us focus on what is central in the moment.

If we sit quietly, just being, clarity often surfaces. However, we have to make the time to settle ourselves down. When we observe our thoughts, feelings, and physical sensations as they happen in the moment, it's like watching water settle after a stone has been thrown in it. Initially, there are many ripples from the commotion. With time, though, the concentric circles gradually fade and are replaced by stillness. Our minds may rarely reach a point of complete rest, but answers often surface from a place of calm.

Re-routing Our Course

When a plane gets off course, it needs to get back on its original route. I love this as an analogy for people because in many ways we're similar to that plane. We too can get back on course if we get off course. We can also change directions if we so decide, or put in different coordinates. And this is so important to keep in mind, because we sometimes fear making decisions, assuming we can't undo our choices. We think the entire outcome of our lives is based on one decision, when in reality no choice is ever truly wrong- it simply provides us with new information, and either takes us further in the direction we want to go or further away from it. As long as we're paying attention, we can always re-route. In fact, sometimes going off the beaten path helps reinforce the direction we most want to take. We learn as we go along and can always change our minds. Who says we have to have it all figured out in advance?

I remember hearing a university academic team tell incoming freshmen years ago, "In a way, it doesn't really matter what you major in. Don't take five years to figure it out or you'll never graduate. Take some time but at some point just make a decision." That stuck with me because it applies to so many things. Sometimes we simply have to take a step; only then we can base our next step on the previous one and whether it turned out well for us or not.

When it comes to making choices, we often seek counsel from others. This can be very helpful to get other people's feedback, or for them to simply reflect back our thoughts so that we see with more clarity. However, we have to be careful when we ask too many people what we should do. At some point we have to have the courage to make our own choices and forge our own paths.

What makes us hesitate in these moments, of course is a lingering fear: "What if I fail? Then who will I have to blame?" The answer is, "absolutely no one." When we make our own choices we have to take full responsibility for our successes and our failures, but at least they are our own. At some point, we have to stop seeking approval and validation from others and approve and validate ourselves, even if we're making things up as we go along. If we mess up, we can always get back on course.

Consulting the Oracle: On Signs, Symbols and Dreams

When we're in profound transformation, we often look for signs- signs for why we're going through something; signs for what we should do; signs for what is going to happen to us. We study our dreams and synchronistic factors trying to determine if there is some hidden, underlying meaning in it all. We ask ourselves: *Is this a coincidence? Or is it a sign from God or the universe telling me what to do or what is to unfold?*

There are times when paying attention in such a way can be incredibly helpful, as information comes in many different forms. But sometimes we have to be comfortable with not knowing as well. Sometimes we can only see a little bit in front of ourselves, and we have to have faith that things will work out.

I also love the role of imagination in plotting our course. We have to be able to visualize what it is we want before we can possibly go about materializing it. Our imaginations are our maps, and our actions are the fuel that propels us to our destinations. I once heard that we must see ourselves as what we want to become versus what we are, and I think that fits in well with active visualization and imagination.

In all of this, it is important to stay open to surprises. Often we are so certain that we know something but then suddenly perceive a different impulse or answer. When this occurs, it can be hard to change gears, particularly if what we perceive seems strange or counter to our rational thoughts. In these situations, it might be helpful to think of the pilots who fly by instruments; they can't see what's ahead, but they have other tools at their disposal to help them find their way.

Chapter 12

Rest

Years ago I read a novel where the lead character described her relationship with her bed as that of a woman with her lover. She was so exhausted that she only longed for her pillow and the peace that would accompany sleep. I remember being amused by her description- but the reality is that it is hard to long for anything but the mattress or couch when we are physically fatigued. In fact, even sexual desire, one of the most basic of human drives, will wane when we're exhausted. The infamous line, "Not tonight honey, I've got a headache," is a common refrain because, quite frankly, many couples are frequently exhausted and therefore "not in the mood" for connection.

In farming there is the tradition of letting fields lie fallow so the soil can replenish itself before planting crops again. For those of us running on empty, burnt out from work and responsibilities that have left us bone tired, we need periods of inactivity. Without pause, it is difficult to get in touch with our innate impulses, particularly when our lives are moving at such a fast pace that we can barely keep up. Transformation then becomes almost impossible.

Rest, therefore, is vital. It is the small flame that will eventually spark into the warmth and strength of desire, productivity, and harvest. If you've ever built a fire, you know that the strike of the match doesn't bring instant results. On the contrary, the fire builds as it is patiently fed with kindling and newspapers. As we sit and watch it grow in intensity, we feel its warmth and the sensual pleasure and comfort it brings. Similarly, when we rest we eventually start to feel joy, inspiration, and motivation return where it might have been nearly extinguished.

Our calendar year is broken into seasons: winter, spring, summer, and fall. But for those of us who don't live in a region where the climate truly dictates what we can and can't do, it's easy to lose track of nature's cycles and rhythms. The show goes on, regardless of the season. Electricity allows us to work until late in the evening, and snow plows clear the roads so we can get to work despite the terrible conditions. So, like the Energizer Bunny, we go and go and go until we reach the brink of collapse.

The problem, of course, is that stretching our limits to the point of breaking serves no one. Pushing ourselves should never bring us to the point of hurting ourselves. We have to develop a level of discernment about when to suck up and push through and when to call it a night. If even God rested on the seventh day, who are we to think that we don't need to as well?

Not only that, when we experience challenges in our lives or suffer great loss, there is a high emotional cost. Processing emotions and integrating life events demands an extreme amount of energy. It is important to acknowledge this and make space for healing. I remember the grieving period after my mom's death consumed one hundred percent of my energy. It was like I had emotional cancer and was receiving chemo: I just needed more time and space to rest than I would normally would. During that period, I made sure to take occasional naps and engage in activities that were replenishing for me.

I am reminded of the story about the goose that lays one golden egg each day. Her owner becomes greedy when he realizes that if she were to lay more than one each day, he'd become wealthy. To this end, he pushes her to lay a greater number of gold eggs- and initially she does. But after a while, she can no longer produce any eggs at all.

I have a dear friend who is incredibly talented and an exceptionally hard worker. Her passion and devotion to her work often leads to her working nonstop. One time she said to me, "Boy did I have a scare. I've been going too many nights with very little sleep. The other day I actually started to hallucinate. It terrified me, and I realized I had to stop everything and get some sleep."

She's not the only person to have had this happen to her. Hallucination is actually a form of psychosis that can occur from not taking care of our basic needs for rest and replenishment.

Without rest, most of us can't think straight. Too much stress and anxiety also impacts thinking. Just the right dose of stress creates the perfect conditions for peak performance levels. When we have too much anxiety present, however, we move away from peak performance mode and into paralysis. We simply shut down. This is why learning to rest and relax is so vital.

When I used to teach psychology at a community college, I'd often tell my students to prepare well leading up to the test, and to simply take it easy and get a good night's rest the night prior. Students who followed this advice tended to do well.

In my office I have a painting of a woman in repose. I actually created the painting myself to remind me of the wonders of rest and relaxation. Because rest is just as vital to my productivity as pushing myself, I found that my office space was the ideal place for that piece of art. Creativity evolves from a tension between will and surrender. We have to know when to push and we have to know when to let go.

When I think of this process, surfing comes to mind. In order to catch a wave, you have to be out in the water paddling in front of the swell. Yet there is this point in which the wave takes you and you stop working and instead allow this magical force to propel you through time and space. Learning to recognize and experience this dynamic balance is an art form- and it is the key to success and transformation. Mastering this invaluable lesson, though, requires a degree of patience.

Most of us want transformation as immediate as a fast food hamburger. Society wants this too. We're supposed to get over pain quickly, immerse ourselves in external activities, and fake it 'til we make it. But these expectations to heal and change quickly haven't always been the norm. There once was a time when it was customary after the death of a loved one to wear black. This signified to the community at large that you were in mourning and needed time to heal, and it usually lasted an entire year. Now when there is a death in the family, most companies allow employees three days off from work to take care of funeral arrangements and grieve. Then folks are expected back at their desk. This is ludicrous. Yet this has become the new line of thinking. If we're not making quick enough progress, we might be offered a medication to expedite it. And while medication can sometimes be helpful temporarily, it can't do the heavy lifting that true transformation requires.

The only way to honor the need for rest in transformation is to claim it for ourselves, because no one else will do that for us. We have to carve out time where we can take care of ourselves instead of waiting for others to give us permission-because they never will. We have to assert our right to a time-out for self-care.

This means that when we're under a considerable amount of pressure and need extra down time, we might tell people that we have other plans when invited to a social event. People don't need to know that those plans are to take a yoga class or go to sleep very early that night. Plans are plans.

When we take this kind of quiet time for ourselves, we make space for the caterpillar within us. We can then dazzle the world with our bright colors again when we emerge feeling more transformed and free. This is how we take flight.

Chapter 13

Not My Circus, Not My Monkeys

Watch any pack of siblings fighting and you'll hear the mom or dad say, "Focus on yourself!" when Sally or John whines, "Mom, he's doing A, B, or C" or "Dad, she's doing X, Y, or Z." We're taught this lesson early on in childhood- yet few of us learn it. It's just so much easier to focus on others and what they are doing: that way, we don't have to take responsibility for ourselves. But it's better to mind our side of the street.

Focusing on others can bring an enormous amount of suffering, particularly when people don't behave the way we want them to. We can express our disappointment and state what we need, but beyond that, we have no control. We can't make others love us, commit to us, or change for us. Nor can we make people be something that they're not, unless they themselves want to change.

When I was growing up, I was deeply worried about my mom's well-being due to her dependence on alcohol. I also worried about my father after he developed a substance use problem as well. But despite all my best intentions, I couldn't get my mom to stop drinking or my dad to stop using drugs. I couldn't prevent my mom from going to jail for five felony DUIs and I couldn't convince her to pursue recovery. And I couldn't prevent my dad from getting disbarred, which ruined his once successful law practice. While I never stopped loving either one of them, I learned that focusing on myself was the only chance I had at serenity.

When we put the focus on ourselves instead of others, we can be perceived as selfish and self-centered. This is unfortunate, because the opposite is true. When we take good care of ourselves, we're actually in a better place to be of service to others. Remember what flight attendants tell passengers before takeoff? "Put your own oxygen mask on first before assisting a child." We need to have enough oxygen ourselves or we aren't of any help to someone else. We also need to discern what we can and can't do to assist someone. Anything else quickly turns into meddling, blaming, controlling, nagging, and manipulating.

Yet it can be seductive to fixate on the problem and how others are perhaps contributing to it- or, from our perspective, causing it. We can get caught up in the latest development of the drama and how someone has betrayed us, let us down, or ruined his or her life and ours. We can become obsessed with the situation and proclaim that we are victims of terrible treatment and misfortune.

I do not want to minimize the tremendous pain involved when we watch loved ones inflict harm on themselves or others. That pain is real and devastating. I have experienced it two-fold with my parents, and there is no way to negate it. Yet because it is so catastrophic and gut-wrenching, we also have to find a way to take care of ourselves even in these terrible situations. Each of us is in our own circus with our own monkeys. We don't need to take on someone else's too- and if our circuses are combined, we need to find a way to focus on our part instead of everyone else's, because that is all we have control over.

Growing up in a home with alcoholism and drug use, I became the consummate observer. I learned how to track the behaviors and moods of others because my survival depended on it. Had my mom been drinking? Was she slurring her words? What level was the vodka in the bottle at? And what was happening with my dad? Was he in a good mood or a bad mood? What pills had he taken today? I learned how to mind everyone else's business but my own.

Focusing on ourselves instead of others can be a hard lesson, particularly if we have a caring and responsible nature. However, it is an important practice, because whenever we put too much focus on others, we take a trip to hell and back- and we suck the breathing space out of our primary relationships too. We need to let people be who they need to be and to find their own way even as we find *our* own way.

All of us, even those of us in union with others, have to live our own lives, and all of us are responsible for our own happiness. One of the most effective ways of ensuring that happiness is to focus on what brings us pleasure and meaning in life. Whenever we find ourselves fixating on others in a compulsive way we can take a personal inventory. Instead of bleeding our energy out in negative ways, we can ask ourselves how we can use our energy creatively. Should we write, paint, or work on a project? Call up a friend? Go for a walk? Pay the bills? Go to the grocery store? We can think about how to contribute to life in a positive way instead of spinning out in our minds about what other people are doing or not doing.

I once went through a romantic break up where my ex-boyfriend started dating a mutual friend three weeks later. They became quite the item immediately, and their new love was documented all over social media. I was devastated by this, despite the fact that he had every right to date whomever he wanted, and despite the fact that these things happen all the time. It felt like a terrible betrayal and a complete dismissal of what we had so recently shared together. Yet I also knew that if I didn't let go of my obsession over what had happened, I would never move on with my life. Letting go didn't mean not grieving or not thinking about the situation. I did plenty of both. But I also trained my thoughts to focus on my own feelings, my own life, and what I was going to do with myself as a newly single woman with no relational prospects on the horizon. It was very challenging for me, because it forced me to confront mid-life issues pertaining to career, community, family, and life goals. But by the end of this excruciating examination, I had made enormous strides in my personal growth and radical changes for the better.

I went to a restorative yoga class once where the teacher made a really interesting comment. "As humans," she said, "we are always pushed into stressful states, yet the body cannot hold stress and relaxation simultaneously. If we train our bodies to relax, it is physiologically impossible to hold stress at the same time. In growth and transformation, there is always a degree of discomfort. So when you hold new poses, you might initially feel uncomfortable."

I burst out laughing at this point, because yeah, growth and transformation can make one a wee bit uncomfortable. That's why it's so much easier to focus on others.

The teacher went on to have us do a pose where we lay on our backs with bolsters and blankets underneath our backs, conforming to our spines in their natural curvatures. She compared our bodies to stones that stay solid and stationary as water runs over them. She explained that water- that ever-pulsating movement of life- can wear down stones, but it doesn't have to push us around. If we remain solid and still, we can be in harmony with the flow of life. I thought this was a particularly helpful way to conceptualize how we can stay grounded in our being despite all that happens in our lives and in relationships with other people. The river will always course around us, but we can stay present with ourselves.

Chapter 14

Restoring Connections

A few summers ago I was teaching in Washington DC and made plans to drive to Williamsburg, Virginia afterwards to visit my grandmother. Right before, news of an approaching hurricane- Hurricane Irene- dominated the news.

Having grown up in California, I was familiar with earthquakes but had never experienced a hurricane. I was in for an adventure.

I arrived at my grandmother's house just as the rain and high winds began to accelerate. I got there just in time; if I had left any later it would have been unsafe to travel and I would have been stuck in a DC hotel for a few more days.

When the storm hit, we lost power and it was dangerous to be on the roads. When things finally settled down a few days later, we drove around the neighborhood to survey the damage. I was surprised to see downed trees with their roots pulled out and fully exposed. I had never seen anything like it. My uncle explained to me that hurricane rains saturate the soil so heavily that the winds easily tear the trees from their roots. Normally so grounded, the trees topple immediately.

During tragedy and loss, we are sometimes like those trees – vulnerable, exposed, and uprooted. Connections with family, friends, or the community at large can be severed and that can make us feel unhinged. When this occurs, we have to find a way to repair the damage and create new connections.

Our connections can be so fragile, though. When I first started working on this book a number of years ago and on this chapter in particular, I remember taking a quick writing break one afternoon. I stretched my legs, made a cup of tea and then clicked onto Facebook to scroll through some of the posts, only to find this breaking news story: in Newtown, Connecticut, at Sandy Hook Elementary School, a gunman had killed twenty young children, and seven adults.

As the news coverage proceeded throughout the following days, the city of Newtown was flooded with support from all over the country. Twenty-seven Christmas trees, wreathes, and ornaments were donated in honor of the lives lost and to help the town decorate during the dark nights of December. Makeshift altars comprised of flowers, teddy bears, cards, and candles sprang up and food and coffee were provided. People across the nation paid their respects in the form of cards, visits, and financial donations. The country was doing what it could to offer its condolences.

A thousand teddy bears, of course, could never fill the holes left in people's hearts after such a profound loss. It takes a tremendous amount of time to heal and is often a lifetime process. But gestures from compassionate strangers *can* help restore our faith in humanity and life. We begin restructuring our lives by honoring the connections being formed in the current moment, even while we are grieving.

Chapter 15

Leaning into Community

As tragedies like Sandy Hook reveal, life can rip the people we care most deeply about away from us in a flash. If and when this happens, we can lose our sense of orientation in the world. But it's not just death that can threaten our primary ties. Loss in any configuration can radically alter how we feel in relation to other people.

It takes community for humans to thrive. We are mammals and mammals always operate in clusters with others of their species. People need people. But what happens when we don't have our loved ones anymore? When our primary relationships come to a natural end or are destroyed?

Now we're in a profound dilemma. We need connection, but our primary social ties have just been obliterated. Reaching out can feel like one more burden that is expected of us when we're already emotionally exhausted. But community doesn't happen passively- so when we're suffering, if we're to survive, we have to develop the capacity to interact with others again, no matter how despondent we feel.

This can be tough. If we've lost someone or something important, we can feel like nothing will ever take its place. We might then reject any kind of connection, because it isn't the one we're mourning. Part of our challenge is to learn how to receive love and kindness from others while still honoring the raw feelings of loss- feelings that might evoke anger, bitterness, and defensiveness when others reach out to us. We have to be careful not to bite the hand that feeds us in our time of need.

The opposite of this scenario is when no meal is offered and it seems like no one cares. This can be excruciating, particularly if we long for connection in whatever form it might take. We can find this unsettling, even shocking- to be alone and have no one reach out to comfort us. When this occurs (and it often does), we suddenly find ourselves at a choice point. We can wallow in despair and grow increasingly isolated and bitter: or, we can smile through our tears and reach out to others, giving them the solace and care we crave for ourselves.

This might sound really unfair. *Why should I reach out to others*, we might think, *when I'm the one who's hurting?* But the reality is, we all need each other. Stepping out of our reality can temporarily soothe our deep loneliness and alter our distorted belief that we will never connect to or belong with others again. It helps reunite us with the human family. Owning our lives will always demand more of us, but it will also never fail to help us grow spiritually.

I'm reminded once again of the Sandy Hook tragedy. A few years after it happened, I had the opportunity to listen to and meet a few of the parents whose lives had been impacted by the shootings. One parent who spoke lost a child. The other parent had a child who had survived but had witnessed the massacre.

I was in awe of those parents' courage and strength- but what impressed me the most was hearing that within a few days of the shooting, the families of Sandy Hook came together to launch a foundation. Called Sandy Hook Promise, the organization helps to "prevent gun violence before it happens by delivering and advocating for mental health and wellness early-intervention programs and by educating the public on gun safety storage practices and sensible state and federal policy." These families were rebuilding connections in almost the same breath that their most precious ones had been obliterated. Even though their hearts had just been broken into a thousand shattered pieces, they were making an effort to connect with other people's hearts.

No One is Alone

Even when solid support systems remain, losses are more often than not experienced privately, without other people knowing the depth of pain we're experiencing. Even when traumas impact an entire community and the nation is aware of them, grief is ultimately metabolized alone. After the camera crews leave and the events become yesterday's news, we're left to pick up the pieces of our lives again. And this can leave us feeling isolated and abandoned.

We shouldn't negate our feelings, but we do have to challenge this notion by realizing that we can connect with ourselves, working to restore places where we may have stepped out of harmony with our inner rhythms. In reestablishing a relationship with the self, we can give ourselves solid ground from which to reach out towards others.

We can also acknowledge that everything bears some relationship with something else- and thus we are never truly alone. We exist within an ecosystem, and we all impact one another. So while we might feel utterly isolated, in reality we are deeply interconnected with everything around us, because we are all part of a much greater whole. Beginning to see the world from this vantage point reminds us that we are in fellowship with others, and that support plays a key role in transformation. Whether help comes from other people or from a reservoir deep within us, it is critical to healing.

It can be helpful to reflect on this sense of unity versus division because our perceptions so influence our well-being. While loss certainly generates sadness and periods of being by ourselves, the idea that we are alone stems from our egos. The ego is the part of the personality that helps structure identity and self-esteem and that mediates between conscious and unconscious thoughts. To do its job, the ego likes to maintain a sense of separation and control. It wants to be number one. In this pursuit, it seeks perfection and competition. But when a terrible loss hits, the ego no longer has control and suddenly doesn't know what to do. It feels like it has to kick into high gear and get back on the job. Likewise, when the ego observes that other people's situations look more appealing than our own, it starts to exert itself through constant comparisons to others, leaving us with feelings of separation and inferiority.

To counter this, we can concentrate on the fact that humans are inherently similar. We are unified by our common needs for connection, meaning, and purpose in life. The more we recognize these truths, the more we heal the schisms in our hearts and can start to feel whole again, whether we're alone or in a room full of people.

Chapter 16

Letting Go of Shame

When my mother was sentenced to time in a state penitentiary, she was transferred from the local prison to Chowchilla, a women's correctional facility in Central California. She was transported in a sheriff's bus that was painted black and white like a zebra, announcing to the world that prisoners were on board. I can feel the humiliation my mother must have experienced. I wonder if she ever talked to any of the other prisoners, or if she slunk down from the window so that no one on the highway could look up and see her. My mother's spirit was as gentle as Bambi's, yet the shame of her alcoholism- and the consequences it led to- eventually compelled her to take her life.

Even if shame doesn't take us to the brink of death, it can weigh on us, impairing our quality of life and hindering our efforts to be authentic, joyful, and vulnerable. It interferes with transformation because it robs us of our courage to step forward, and while it might not kill the body, it can kill our vitality and spirit.

By itself, shame is simply an emotion meant to alter our behavior in some way. Without shame, we would never check our impulses and might run the risk of being kicked out of our family, village, or tribe due to unrestrained behavior. Yet if we get stuck in it, suffering from shame becomes like swimming with our clothes on. The weight will exhaust us.

Think of a young child experimenting with her vocal chords. There is nothing wrong or sinful with a toddler making noise. Yet to the adults in the room, the racket she is making can be irritating and disruptive. Thus, as she gets older and develops language to express her needs, adults start to censor the spontaneous noises she makes. Chances are, she is shushed or scolded at times, and as a result, she might feel shame.

When we're little, we lack the cognitive development to understand why we are being scolded, laughed at, or told to stop doing something. Thus, we often internalize the shame we feel in these situations, and we equate it with being bad ourselves. This is very different from guilt which stems from doing something deemed as wrong or that would hurt someone. Shame is a feeling that we are somehow flawed even when we haven't done anything bad. While guilt helps us develop a sense of right or wrong, shame can become problematic. We may overidentify with it and internalize it in unhealthy ways.

I believe my mom lived with a deep sense of shame from an early age. In fact, she probably started drinking to numb her shame. But the more she drank, the more her shame intensified. She felt embarrassed by her inability to control herself- felt that her alcoholism and depression made her fundamentally flawed. When her drinking led to driving under the influence, she then felt guilty for breaking the law. Shame led to guilt, and guilt reinforced shame. These two feelings often go hand in hand.

Chapter 17

Transforming Shame

In life we go from moment to moment trying to escape our vulnerability. We attempt to protect our happiness, safety, and comfort. And when something happens that interferes with our well-being, we often attribute this to personal failure or a deep flaw within. While we have no reason to blame ourselves, the inherent vulnerability we feel when trauma strikes often triggers shame.

As my life unfolded, shame became like an old, familiar coat for me- one I wore throughout childhood and well into adulthood. I perceived myself as flawed because of my parents' struggles and wondered if on some level I was bad. I also had an increasing sense that life was like a video game where missiles of misfortune could decimate me at every turn. I felt impotent because I couldn't fix things and didn't understand that circumstances were beyond my control- to the extent that when a cop pulled my mother and me over because of her drinking, I felt like *I* was the one in trouble. I also remember kids laughing because my mom's behavior seemed so strange. Once, while intoxicated, she inadvertently lit her fingernail on fire while trying to light a match. In that moment, I wished I were invisible.

Shame that occurs when things happen beyond our control runs deep. It reminds me of the childhood tale "The Ugly Duckling." In the story, a swan egg rolls into a nest of duck eggs. Upon hatching, the swan looks so different from the others that he is ridiculed and referred to as the "Ugly Duckling." The swan has done nothing wrong, but because he is so ostracized, he is filled with profound shame.

I imagine the Ugly Duckling initially assumed the other ducks would love him, and this made his disillusionment all the more painful. We encounter the same grief when we suffer unexpected disappointment. Whether our lover betrays us, a family member dies, or our retirement savings gets wiped out in a day, unanticipated traumas leave us feeling as if the rug has been pulled out from underneath us. Then, when our ideas about love or life don't measure up, we can feel ashamed that our perceptions of security proved false. We might also feel that those who failed us should feel remorse for their contributions to our misfortune. All of a sudden, we realize the perceptions we once had cannot guarantee control and this can feel utterly terrifying. In this way, shame represents an essential wound that we all wrestle with throughout our lives.

Like a weed threatening to destroy other plant life, shame can suffocate us and inhibit our transformation. That's why we have to build up shame resiliency. But in order to transcend shame, we have to face our own vulnerability and imperfection with love, courage, and a persistent focus on the changes we want to make. It also helps to feel accepted unconditionally by someone who believes in us.

There is a belief in many religious traditions that humans are made in the image of God and carry an aspect of the Divine. It can be comforting to believe that while we are also deeply flawed in some ways, nothing can change that aspect of us which is pure and good. Part of healing from shame involves reflecting on this part of our nature, sometimes referred to as the "Imago Dei."

It can also be helpful to challenge our shameful thoughts by asking, "Is this really true? Am I really x, or y, or z?" If we're feeling deep shame, however, we might not be able to automatically release that feeling, even if we know our thoughts are distorted. If this is the case, we might try a slightly different approach. We might want to try shifting our focus away from shameful thoughts and instead try dwelling on things that bring us a sense of peace and wholeness. When we put increased energy on good things, sometimes the paralyzing feelings of shame start to neutralize. For instance, if we go for a walk in nature or play with an animal or child, we start to focus more on the present moment than on how bad we think we are or the mistakes we've made. The more we fill ourselves up with a sense of the Divine in life, the more we eclipse the darker feelings that want to take away our light. We can gently remind ourselves that we are all human and trying the best that we can.

The reality is, whether we're perfect or not, not everyone will like us! We do not have to apologize for breathing or for being ourselves. Everything on this planet is deserving of love and respect– including each of us! When we embrace love and compassion, the shame starts to fade away and we begin to transform our lives. We are all here for a purpose– to let our lights shine. We serve no one by shrinking ourselves and hiding our gifts from the world.

Chapter 18

Surrender and Will

Do you ever find yourself grasping for control, love, or acceptance? Have you ever tried to wrangle life or relationships as if they were animals you could tame or bend to your will? If so, you've probably realized at some point that life and relationships are things over which we have very little control- and you've ended up frustrated.

So often in life, we want to call the shots. We're taught in our individualistic society that we can do anything and everything- that we can conquer the world. But pushing too hard can be a setup for disaster. When we operate this way, we often become rigid, exhausted, and unpleasant to be around. It is only when we surrender that a softness returns and we can find a balance between our strengths and vulnerabilities.

Surrender is key, but how do we learn this if all we've known is trying to manage things on our own?

Years ago, I worked with emotionally disturbed children. Some of them had been so abused that it was common for them to struggle with containing angry impulses. When upset, they would sometimes pick up objects and hurl them across the room, bite peers, or bang their heads against the wall.

I remember watching a very upset little boy. He was no older than four. Our music and drama therapy session was ending and he was quite sad, but he didn't know how to process his feelings about the play coming to a close. When my co-therapist and I told him that in five minutes we would begin to pack up the instruments, he began to run around the room in circles, and then he picked up a trashcan and threw it. My co-therapist talked to the boy gently, and told him to stop. When this yielded no results, my colleague calmly picked up the child and brought him to his lap. Only then did the child stop acting angry and begin to cry, saying he didn't want to leave the music/drama group. He was having too much fun.

Perhaps we could all benefit from being held in the strong, loving arms of someone bigger than us, when we feel the urge to rage about all the things that have gone wrong in our lives. If we let God hold us, it might soothe the broken, skittish parts of ourselves.

We want to fight, but it is far wiser to surrender. In surrender, there is power.

The other day, a rose in a lovely bouquet I had on my table fell from its stem. Rather than toss it out, I placed it in a mason jar full of water, remembering how my grandmother used to create gorgeous flower arrangements sustained in water alone. Sure enough, once contained in the safety of glass and water, the rose started to thrive. Instead of dying, the blossom remained strong for a number of days.

Sometimes when falling to the ground with petals wide open, we end up doing just fine. In this free fall, we often radiate our essence.

One of the best ways to conceptualize surrender is to think about our breathing. When we allow ourselves to breathe fully, we practice this act with every exhalation. When we instead hold our breath, we are doing the opposite; we are interrupting the natural process of letting go, gripping with our muscles, and restricting our bodies' natural flow of energy.

We breathe automatically, of course, whether or not stress causes us to restrict our breath. But the more consciousness we bring to our breathing process, the more we assist ourselves in letting go of stress. This also helps us to release thoughts and emotions that might be stagnating in our bodies.

So often when bad things happen in our lives we put up a major fuss. We want to prevent what is happening from happening, because who wants to experience heartache and challenge? This is such a natural reaction. We all do it. And it is almost a form of denial; if we just pretend that the cancer isn't spreading or try to be perfect so that our spouse will end his or her affair, then maybe we can prevent the excruciating pain. Unfortunately, all our best efforts at control often fail miserably and make things worse. Acceptance is often the first step towards peace and transformation.

To help navigate the balance between surrender and will, we might look to the serenity prayer: "God, grant me the serenity to accept the things I cannot change, the courage to change the things I can, and the wisdom to know the difference." There are certain things we simply cannot change, and the sooner we realize this the better. Trying to change what can't be changed is like hitting our heads against a wall over and over again, to the point of bleeding. It reflects a persistent stubbornness and refusal to accept reality. We try to exert our will where we really have no business doing so.

On the other hand, there are things that we absolutely can do to improve our life situations. To not do so is to play the victim and to invite catastrophe into our lives. The key, then, is to know what we can and can't do, and to act accordingly.

There is an organic, natural flow to transformation when we suit up, show up, and go about our business while also allowing life's circumstances to evolve without our manipulations. If we allow events the breathing space to unfold in their own unique ways, we can be surprised by the outcomes that occur free of our meddling.

When I was a young girl my chores consisted of a considerable amount of gardening. I learned right away that flowers bloom on their own timetables and that plants can't be forced to grow. They simply need care. I also had no control over when blossoms withered. Petals would fall to the ground when their time came. But alongside those dying flowers new buds would spring forth. My job then was to pull off the dead leaves because this made space for new growth.

While it's true that this constant cycle of transformation involves a sense of dying, it also brings new life. Like the phoenix, the mythical bird that continually rises from its own ashes, we too can rejuvenate after loss. Without an understanding of this, we lose tremendous opportunities for growth. We have to be willing to let go and to let parts of ourselves die so other parts of ourselves can blossom.

The healing process is never really something we can fully control. We can't pencil in grief on our calendars and think that after that appointed hour, we'll be done with the process. We have to allow healing to move on its own timetable, and to adjust our energy levels and actions accordingly. In a way, this is like allowing a river to run its course instead of trying to dam up the water.

When we stop trying to fight the currents, they eventually transform. Nothing can stay the same forever. Thoughts, feelings, sensations, and circumstances eventually shift and change into something else as we navigate the balance between taking action in our lives and inviting stillness.

If you've ever studied dancing, you know that it takes considerable focus, patience, and discipline to learn the techniques and the choreography. Only after these have been mastered can the dancer surrender fully to the music and experience consummate freedom within her prescribed movements. Structure is inherent in dance, even when it appears effortless- but at the same time, the dancer who clings rigidly to the steps and fails to let go even a little bit misses out on some of the joy and liberation of dance. Dance is a blend of effort and surrender- a quality that makes it a wonderful metaphor for life.

I wonder if the driving force behind our tendencies to control things stems from fear more than anything else. I wonder if there would be less of a need to control external chaos if we felt safer and had a sense of unity with life. I'm reminded of the trust fall exercise I've experienced in group settings. In the exercise, a person stands on the edge of a table and then leans back, allowing a bunch of ready and steady hands to brace their fall. This requires consummate trust that the group will be there to catch you. And they always are. What would it be like if we could trust that in surrender, the fall is always braced by grace?

Chapter 19

Realigning Priorities

Transformation requires a high degree of focus. We have to know who we want to become or our metamorphosis will be somewhat haphazard- or it won't happen at all. While we don't have to have everything one hundred percent figured out, we do need to become clear on what is important to us. If we don't, we'll get swept along with no control over our own lives. Before we know it, our lives will be over, and we'll wonder what happened.

There are a thousand things that can distract us from our sense of purpose in life. And when we don't know our purpose or what we value, we become even more susceptible to being seduced away from the things we'd like to pursue or accomplish.

Years ago I read the book *Seven Habits of Highly Effective People* by Stephen Covey, and I was struck by one of the concepts introduced in the book: Covey suggests that people schedule their tasks around what matters most to them first. If we put what is most important to us at the bottom of the list, he says, it will always remain at the bottom. Neglected. What needs to get done finds a way to get done when we put our priorities first.

Not only do we lose track of time when we randomly go about our days without putting our values in order, many of us also lose sight of our mission or purpose. In fact, many of us don't even know what our mission or purpose is to begin with. When we experience hardship, however, we sometimes reach a crossroads that compels us to decide what matters to us.

As I mentioned in the chapter on boldness, when I was a young girl I had a strong sense that I was supposed to have a creative career as an actor and filmmaker. But after graduating from college I became afraid of pursuing my passions. My parents' problems loomed large, and it was hard to think about chasing my dreams when their lives seemed so unhappy. Although I continued studying acting and writing screenplays, I took my career in a vastly different direction. There was nothing wrong with my decision to work in mental health: it was a wonderful use of some of my skills, and it allowed me to contribute positively to other people's well-being. But there was an aspect of my life that remained unfulfilled.

Then, in my late forties, when I experienced the painful romantic breakup I mentioned in a previous chapter, I had to reevaluate my life direction. I was forty-six, and suddenly I was forced to come to terms with the fact that the life I had imagined for myself did not seem to be manifesting. I was faced with a deep internal question: What did I want from life if I wasn't going to become a wife and mother?

I picked up a book from my bookshelf by acting coach Larry Moss called *Intent to Live*. Although the book's content is specific to the craft of acting, it also talks much about how a creative life feeds our passions. In the span of an hour, I was calling a cinematographer friend of mine who'd been encouraging me to shoot a short film based on a feature I'd written. I had pushed away his promptings for years while the script sat on my bookshelf gathering dust. But now I was ready. I needed to do something outlandish that would wake up my heart to the beat it used to know. Within a few months I was on a film set in LA- and shortly afterward, I moved there. The experience gave me new direction and realigned my priorities.

It is important to know what our priorities are and what we want in life. If we don't know, we should start asking questions. If we don't, other people will decide for us. They'll tell us who we are and what we should be doing. They will not be concerned with our needs: they will define our lives by who they need us to be. And this is not a healthy way to live.

We are meant to use our gifts and we are meant to contribute to the world. We are also meant to express our joy and to live our own lives as we define them. This is not selfish. It is actually generous. It allows us to shine our light and to come from a place of wholeness, which in and of itself generates love and compassion. When we're miserable, we're hardly helpful to others.

When we move closer to owning our lives, there is a complete realignment in our being. Our work can change, our relationships can change, and our very demeanor can change. This can be both thrilling and terrifying, because as we get focused, other people might not understand what we're up to. They might criticize us or try to deter us. They might be jealous or resentful because we're following our hearts and perhaps they aren't following theirs. Keep on trucking anyway!

Our priorities don't necessarily have to be goal oriented, although they can be. More essentially, our priorities reflect our values and our passions. We can ask ourselves, what is it that we value? Relationships? Health? Time spent in nature? Volunteering and helping in various organizations? With only so many hours in the day, how do we want to spend our free time? And with so many hours spent at work, how can we find work that is meaningful and enjoyable?

Taking ownership of our lives requires courage. It is easier to stick to the status quo so that we never have to risk the realities of both success and failure. When we align with our priorities, we sometimes have to prune away things that no longer matter as much as they used to. This requires the type of commitment we see in Olympic athletes, or even in devoted parents. We might have to drop certain activities, say no when we used to say yes or say yes when we used to say no, and discipline ourselves in new ways. This is by no means easy, but it allows us to completely live our own lives.

We do not have to be like everyone else and we do not have to be liked by everyone. We can define how we structure our chores, social life, family life, and work life. While it's true that there are always obligations in life that we have to adhere to, we have significantly more choices than we realize.

I remember working in an organization years ago where no one seemed to take the lunch hour they were legally allotted. Everyone ate at their desks and complained about how much work they had to do. There was indeed much work to be done, but I chose to take my hour to go swimming. A public pool was close by and I'd rush over and quickly do some laps. Then I'd eat my sandwich in the car and return to the office with wet hair. People would give me the evil eye when I walked in, but I didn't care enough to stop taking my lunch this way. My health was important to me, and spending time outside in the fresh air raised my spirits. It also increased my productivity when I returned to work, because I felt relaxed and clear-headed after swimming.

When we embrace our priorities, we care less about what others think about us and focus more on what makes us happy, healthy, and whole. And just as important, we quietly give other people permission to do the same.

Chapter 20

Logging Onto Something Else

When I was in middle school and high school I was expected to get up at 5:30 a.m. to water the plants and take care of our animals before going to school at 8:00 a.m. This was in Southern California, where delicate potted plants needed to be watered in both the morning and late afternoon. Much of our shrubbery had automatic drip-and-spray sprinklers, but the plants that didn't would easily die within a few days without consistent care, particularly the orchids and fuchsias, which are fragile, moisture-loving flowers. These varieties are tropical in nature and not meant for an arid, dry climate.

These days many of us log onto the computer or our phones to check text messages and emails the minute we wake up. There is little division anymore between work and private life. It's all mushed into one undifferentiated mass. And if we're not careful, technology can take us completely out of ourselves, making genuine transformation more challenging.

I'd rather water plants at 5:30 a.m. and walk and brush two large, magnificent dogs as I did when I was young than look at a screen the minute I open my eyes. It's a more humane way to wake up. It's more embodied; more centered; more intimate. It's semi-equivalent to a toddler jumping on your bed or a lover kissing you awake. When outdoors at 5:30 a.m., you see the sunrise and the way the colors shift with an ever- increasing degree of light.

Sometimes we have to say no to work and to technology. This actually feeds productivity, because relaxation restores the mind and soul. It opens new vistas. Yet this isn't just about rest. This is about logging into our inner lives. Taking internal time is essential for growth and helps reinforce our strength and vitality.

When I was that high school student up early each morning, it was the era of Nancy Reagan's "Just say no!" campaign to help young people not succumb to drug use. I think of that phrase now. As direct as Nike's "Just do it!", "Just say no!" is a great motto- if you can adhere to it. It can help us unplug from technology.

I once heard addiction described as anything that takes us out of ourselves. I thought that was a really interesting definition that made a lot of sense. When under the influence of drugs or alcohol, we're not present. And the same can be said of many other things that can lure us away from the moment and being conscious.

Technology and social media have many positive uses: if we're continually connected to such sources, however, using them can become addicting. Being on Facebook or Twitter or Instagram nonstop can become all about documenting our lives instead of actually living them. Likewise, fixating on other people's lives by stalking their pages can rob us of being present in our own existence. When we're in the midst of profound change, it can be helpful to focus more on our lives than on what everyone else out there is doing. The latter invites constant comparisons to others and can induce a high-school mentality where we're highly influenced by the dominant groups and "in" people. This can completely bleed out our energy.

In yoga there is a position called "tree pose." To get into the position, you lift one leg up and place it on your knee while lifting your arms above your head. Basically it is a posture to build strength and balance. To maintain stability and not teeter, you press your standing leg into the floor and engage your muscles, helping your body maintain a gravitational center. You also focus on one point on the wall in front of you to avoid any visual distractions that might cause your head to turn and thus offset your body's balance.

Tree pose is a great metaphor for life. In order to maintain stability and balance, we have to draw on strength, will and focus. This keeps us emotionally and mentally solid in our day-to-day existence. Otherwise, anything can offset our equilibrium. I liken this to a real-life tree that remains firmly rooted even when the wind and rain blow its leaves and branches about.

When there are too many distractions and we're not in alignment, we are not rooted. Television, cell phones, music, everyone talking at the same time and multi-tasking can split our focus, especially if we're bombarded by too much of this all at once.

When I was a little girl I visited my grandparents in Wisconsin every summer. I have extremely fond memories of my experiences there- primarily because my grandparents were so focused on me while I was visiting. Because their lives had a degree of balance, there was a spaciousness that allowed them to be dialed in to my life as a child. We all sat down and ate dinner together every night, and typically went for a walk afterwards. We were logged into our family relationships as opposed to everyone sitting at the table (or in different rooms) on our devices. (Of course, the devices I'm referring to didn't exist then).

When our focus becomes scattered and we're fixated on too many external things, we can try to make our focus more inward rather than more outward. We can narrow the sphere of our relationships and activities to what is manageable instead of trying to be all things to all people all the time. Doing so requires a form of self-sufficiency that harkens back to times when we didn't have such easy access to communication and to each other. While it can be invaluable to seek connection and support with others, it can also be invaluable to sit in silence and connect with our inner selves first.

As I mentioned in an earlier chapter, I lived in Bandung, Indonesia for a year as an exchange student when I was eighteen. Upon arrival I immediately began attending Indonesian school six days a week, though I spoke very little Indonesian. I had much to learn about living in a culture so distinctly different from my own. There were days when I felt incredibly alone in my experience, because of the language barrier and because everything was so unfamiliar to me. Before I got more settled, I often felt awkward and anxious.

I think back on that time and realize that the only communication I had with family and friends in America was letters *par avion*. Snail mail. And letters could take fourteen days to arrive. There was no Internet or email or Facebook. Cell phones didn't exist yet either, so telephoning America was too expensive. I only talked with my mom once on the phone during my entire year there. Because of my isolation, I had to log into the life around me in order to fit in, and I had to log into myself to figure things out. I also dialed into journal writing and my own version of spirituality. I wonder if I could do that now. What would it be like to have to be fully present with myself and the people in my immediate surroundings instead of focused vastly out?

Transformation demands that we do things differently in our lives. It asks that we step out of our comfort zones and into new situations. It requires that we be present and dialed into our lives. Whatever steps we need to take to do this is essential. We have to figure out who, what, when and where we want to be logged onto that enhances our fullest expression of growth and wellbeing. We might consider looking at the sunset or full moon directly instead of searching for it on the Internet. That way we'll be sure to see it live and not miss the real deal.

Chapter 21

Attitudes of Gratitude

When we hit turbulence in life we most definitely experience rough feelings- and those emotions become even more complex over time as our memory banks begin to associate certain experiences (whether positive or negative) with particular emotions. These associations influence how we react to thoughts and feelings in the present.

To transform our wounds into gifts, we have to somehow make peace with our feelings. We can't ignore the difficult emotions: nor can we wallow in them or allow them to be the only one with voices. We somehow have to honor all of our feelings and see how they may or may not inform our thoughts and behaviors.

Gratitude can be the way to navigate this complex terrain.

When we process difficult emotions, people can accuse us of being negative. It can seem as if we're anything but grateful. This is because it is easy to confuse negative emotions with negative attitudes. In reality, though, emotions and attitudes are distinctly different. We can feel very sad about something, yet still have an overall positive outlook on life.

It's common to confuse emotions and attitudes because all of us attach thoughts to feelings, and sometimes these thoughts can be extremely negative. Instead of taking a situation at face value, we can attribute false ideas to it. For instance, if someone is upset with me about something, I might feel bad and attach a number of distorted beliefs to my feelings. I might think, *I'm bad, no one likes me, I always screw things up.* Now I have paired negative thoughts with sad feelings. The more I fixate on these thoughts, the more my sadness will increase. The irony is, the person upset with me probably doesn't think these thoughts in relation to me. They are probably just upset about the circumstances, and still care about me despite their feelings of anger or hurt.

Sad feelings do not create negativity: the thoughts we ruminate on do. Thus, we must challenge whether our thoughts are true or not. Thinking constructively when painful feelings emerge helps us better tolerate difficult emotions. While this might sound like work, the work is worth it for the emotional elasticity- the deeper capacity to experience love and joy- that accompanies it. If we censor our emotional expression, then there isn't much room for positive feelings to flow through, either. It's ultimately best to keep the heart hub as open as we can, because doing so allows us to experience all the wonderful things life has to offer.

As we do this, we can also cultivate an attitude of gratitude. Like folding an ingredient into a cake batter, gratitude tempers what is already in the bowl. It helps us smooth out the bitter feelings and concentrate on happiness and strength. Instead of focusing on all that is wrong in our lives, we can counter negative realities with some of our blessings. This isn't about negating genuine emotion, being in denial, or adopting a Pollyanna persona. This is simply about integrating gratitude into our healing process while also staying present with parallel realities. It's a way of expanding perspective. Like extending the camera back for a full shot instead of staying in close-up. The view is different depending on the angle.

We're always better off when we can take a ten-thousand-foot view and see things from a different vantage point. I love flying for this reason. I enjoy seeing the entire landscape- a view that I don't have access to when I'm on the ground.

Whenever we're mired in complexity or difficult life events, we can ask ourselves, *What is working in our lives? What do we have to be grateful for? Where might there be a silver lining in the story?*

While they certainly don't qualify as tragedies, car problems always challenge me to see the big picture and to stretch my gratitude muscles. When my car requires repairs, my knee-jerk reaction is to be upset. I complain and worry about the cost and become irritated.

Then, however I pause and focus on the wonder of my vehicle and how it serves me. I also think about how profoundly lucky I've been whenever my car has broken down. I recall a time when I pulled up in front of my house one evening after work- and just as I drove up to the curb, my engine went dead. When that happened, I immediately went into collapse mode. It had been a brutally long day. This was the last thing I needed to deal with. I was exhausted and I was moving to Los Angeles in a week. I had so looked forward to finally relaxing that evening and now I was all keyed up again.

Then I thought, *Thank God my car died right in front of the house and not on the freeway.*

In the morning I had the car towed to the mechanic right down the street. The repairs were very expensive but included general maintenance that I knew was soon due anyway. The bill did not please me, yet I saw the grace in the whole event. I was moving to Los Angeles, the land of freeways and traffic and my car had died right beforehand- and got the full spa treatment as a result. Now it was in good shape for the adventure it was about to embark upon. Not only that, the auto repair place had a unique service of washing vehicles after they were serviced. My car was filthy, and I'd been way too busy to wash it myself. It had been bugging me for weeks. As they pulled the car around for me to pick up, there it was, gleaming and sparkling clean. I smiled like a proud mother and realized that in the greater scope of life, this was small-potatoes stuff.

Gratitude helps us keep things in perspective and remember that there is suffering in the world much greater than our own. In this case, I realized I was lucky to own a vehicle at all.

In this example, all my feelings were real: I was irritated, tired, cranky, and fearful about what was wrong with my car before the diagnosis, among other things. But when I took a moment to focus on gratitude, I was able to see the situation much differently.

One of the benefits of cultivating gratitude is that it encourages us to take time to acknowledge a degree of abundance in our lives. Even in the heart of deep sorrow and misfortune, it's possible to embrace blessings. We might have a terrible day wrought with hardship, but we can still look outside the window and see a deer on the lawn or step outside and feel a ray of warm sunshine gracing our face. These are small, everyday miracles that can ease the spirit like the proverbial balm in Gilead. However, an attitude of gratitude requires conditioning, just as muscles do. We have to take time to look around, become aware, and actively acknowledge good things in our lives.

Entitlement is the opposite of gratitude, and unfortunately we live in a society rampant with this characteristic. Ours is a nation of such blessings and prosperity that many of us, myself included, often forget what impoverished conditions other humans in the world suffer through on a daily basis. There are people in this world dying of hunger, ravaged by violence in their communities, and impacted by disease, tainted water, and poor medical care. We might pause when we are complaining about not having enough or things being bad to think about how bad life really could be.

That's not to say our problems, feelings, and concerns aren't legitimate. They are. It's just that sometimes we have to step back and see things from a more global view. We can honor our hardships and give thanks for our blessings simultaneously. For example, we can give thanks for our food before we eat. Even if we are not thanking a God, we can thank the individuals who planted, harvested, and cooked what is on our plate. We can see the tremendous natural beauty on this planet and steward it instead of savagely destroying it through greed. And we can honor those around us who, through a smile or kind gesture, make our lives better. When we practice attitudes of gratitude, personal transformation is inevitable.

Chapter 22

Practice Creates Opportunities

When a young child is learning to walk, she doesn't automatically go from crawling to standing. Instead she drags herself up while holding onto a chair or a table, and then she cautiously takes a step while still grasping the furniture. Next, she lifts her hands off from whatever she was clinging to for support and takes another step. Then she falls flat on her behind.

No matter how many times children stumble in their attempts to walk, they determinedly keep trying. The allure of mobility beckons, plus they have no history of failure. They bravely persevere.

Unfortunately, by the time we reach adulthood, we have a whole memory bank of disappointments and hurts. Because of this, as we recover from life's blows, taking steps out on our own might be scary. It can be hard to trust the process. But like the young child learning to walk, we too must persevere.

It's helpful to think about how much learning happens through both exploration and mistakes. Failures are often critical to success. We learn what works by figuring out what doesn't work.

Likewise, is there such a thing as perfect? And do we even want it? The quest for perfection can kill freedom, spontaneity, and creativity.

My acting teacher often says, "It's your job to throw up. The editor will clean it up." In essence, it's important to allow impulses to flow openly– the good, the bad, and the ugly. Indeed, in film acting, there are many takes, and the editor shapes the takes accordingly. If there is a bad take, it doesn't matter; there are twenty more for the editor to choose from.

Yoga follows a similar principle. I once heard a yoga teacher say, "There is no such thing as perfect in yoga. The minute you think you have perfection the moment will be gone. Then you open again to the not knowing, the fumbling, the tension, and the pushing. Then you find it again, but only for a moment. That's why we call it a practice. The beauty, though, is that the practice creates possibilities. Without a practice, everything shrinks. There are few possibilities."

I am reminded over and over again that we need to practice "being" in the midst of doing, and that when we engage in the "practice" of rest and relaxation, many opportunities emerge from the resulting spaciousness. It's a constant tension between being and doing, process and product, will and surrender. And it is our breath and spirit that will sustain us through these explorations. It is always the journey that gets us to the eventual destination: it is never about the destination itself.

Everything is a practice. It's not just things we're striving to master such as an art form or an academic subject. Our very lives become a practice. While we may strive for certain outcomes, such as happiness or kindness or enjoying life to the fullest, in the process we ultimately practice the art of being. Some days we are not happy but instead are sad. Then the practice is not so much about being happy or sad but rather noticing what we are feeling. In this way we develop curiosity and compassion for our process. We practice observing our ups and downs, our breath, and our feelings. When we show up fully present in our lives each day, we set the stage for magic to occur. Doors open when we seek and knock.

A few years back, I surfed nearly every day. If you want to learn about "practice," I highly recommend taking up the sport, because you will have many opportunities to be pummeled by waves and thrown off your board while waiting to catch that one delicious ride. It is a lesson in humility and patience. Yet when you catch a wave there is truly nothing like it. It is every cliché in the book. When people say surfing is so "spiritual," they aren't kidding.

That said, each time you paddle out, you never know what the conditions will be like. One morning I went out and the waves were really choppy. Due to the wind and something about the ocean currents I still don't understand, it was hard to catch anything. As I sat on my board feeling the waves lap about, I felt more like I was on a boat than a surfboard. Yet there we all were– half of San Diego, sitting there and hoping that something would come along and break cleanly.

I had been out the day before, when the conditions were perfect, and I'd caught wave after wave after wave in gentle succession. Now, as I sat there waiting for a single decent wave to come my way, I suddenly realized that sometimes we just get lucky; sometimes the conditions are ideal. And when they aren't, there isn't a whole lot we can do about it.

As the morning progressed, the conditions didn't change, but every now and then a swell formed on the horizon that showed promise- and every time that happened, all of us in the lineup took our positions: noses pointing toward shore, bellies on boards, toes slightly curled, paddling, paddling, paddling. And then a random few of us were blessed enough to be in the right place at the right time. Similar to when a plane taxis on the runway and builds momentum until takeoff, surfers know when their efforts and a wave's power have created enough synergy to allow them to stand and ride.

That day, another surfer caught a wave at the same time I did, and we rode it side by side. As we both got back on our boards, he asked, "Did you enjoy that wave?"

I nodded.

"I did too," he said, "and we both got to ride it. Praise God!"

I thought about his praise for God. It struck me that none of us are omnipotent. I, at least, have learned that I don't have full power to make things happen in my life just because I try to will them into being. I know that for every wave I catch, one can viciously knock me down. So, yes, I'll acknowledge blessings that happen to come my way.

When I used to surf regularly, there were days when I totally wiped out. Sometimes it was my fault. I'd be tired or not paying attention, and would just do stupid things. Sometimes I'd be grandiose about my capabilities and would take risks I shouldn't. Other times, however, I simply fell victim to the ocean's currents. When that was the case, I did my best to work with the conditions to stay out of harm's way.

As time went on, I learned that in order to catch a wave, it was essential to suit up, get in the water, and paddle out. It was critical to be out there, to practice, and to be ready, even on the days when the waves didn't look promising.

Because riding a wave all the way to shore is the most beautiful thing.

Chapter 23

Take the Feeding

This year, I've watched two friends go through divorces. Even to the observer, the pain of this is excruciating. As I've listened, I've witnessed each friend struggle with accepting his new reality.

All humans resist dramatic change. We kick and scream when we see it coming, and howl when we have no control. How can it be that what was once so certain and part of our day-to-day life is now gone? How can affections be here today and gone tomorrow? Why does the sun rise and set? Why does life include pain, and why do good things have to end?

I have absolutely no answers to these questions. I only know that from the outside looking in, we cause ourselves tremendous pain when we refuse to let go- when we expect things to be different than the way they are- because we have no control over people, places, and things. The only thing we have control over is ourselves.

Years ago I heard a phrase that beautifully sums up our very human tendency to effect change in places we can't: "You can't get bread from a hardware store."

Whenever we want someone to give us something that he or she simply isn't capable of giving, we have to remind ourselves that we're shopping in the wrong place. The hardware store is not bad because it doesn't provide bread. In fact, if we're working on a home improvement project, the hardware store is great! But if we're hungry, we need to find a bakery or grocery store.

The Courage to Ask and the Courage to Receive

Even though we may feel alone when wading through rough waters, ultimately, we need to seek support from others- which always means risking our vulnerability. While it's true we have no control over others, we can learn to be more discerning about whom we can rely on and ask for support. Because the reality is, many people want to be of service. For all those that are not available, there are many others who are.

What, then, stops us from seeking support? Is it that we're afraid of rejection? Are we concerned people will not understand our pain or perhaps be frightened by it? Is it that we feel like no one can make the pain go away, so why hope for any kind of relief?

Whatever our concerns and previous disappointments, asking for support is vital. If we don't, we'll eventually starve. When we are grieving or struggling, we need understanding and companionship. Community offers us that nourishment. Yet sometimes we dismiss the compassion and assistance others offer us because it doesn't come in the package we were expecting or most desiring. This is like refusing to eat a sandwich because we want filet mignon instead. This type of refusal also inhibits others from sharing gifts with us.

Sometimes, of course, we need quiet and to be alone. I'm not saying we have to respond to anything and everything people offer. What I am saying, however, is that if we always refuse help, we will eventually become lonely, tired, angry, alienated, and exhausted.

Most people want to help in a crisis situation. When this is what we desire, we must humble ourselves and ask for what we need, because few humans are mind readers. It is a rare moment when individuals do the perfect thing without our indicating what might help us. It is better to communicate clearly; in that way, we can avoid resentment and unrealistic expectations.

On the other hand, people do sometimes surprise us with their uncanny ability to know exactly what we need. The first anniversary of my mother's death was such a time. I remember that I was coming home from work that day, exhausted from trying to hold it all together, and as I approached my front door, I noticed a box.

I hadn't ordered any books from Amazon. Perplexed, I picked up the package. The label indicated the sender was a florist. I opened the cardboard flaps and discovered an exquisite bouquet of roses tucked away inside. The flowers, beautifully preserved by the delicate packaging, peered up at me. I looked at the enclosed card. They were from my best friend. She was out of the country at the time, but she had remembered the anniversary of my mom's death and wanted me to feel supported. The kind gesture, and the realization that I hadn't been forgotten, brought me to tears.

An Ethereal Form of Support

While we might think connections with loved ones completely break when relationships end or aren't working, we sometimes discover that ties transcend time, space, and geography. Not only that, our perspectives may shift with time. Insights can emerge as unexpected gifts later on.

In my case, by the time I was in my late thirties, my mom and I had a limited relationship. So much grief and loss had ensured in the years leading up to her death that my heart had closed on some levels. Yet the period after her death revealed that we'd had a much closer and more complex bond than I'd ever realized or appreciated. This generated a considerable amount of healing and transformation for me.

One such example of this occurred about a year and half after my mom died. I was on a trip to Big Sur and Carmel- a part of the country my father loved, and that my family used to go to on vacation every year. Long ago, when my mom was pregnant, he was stationed at Fort Ord and she visited him there before they officially moved out West from Wisconsin.

The house I stayed at during my vacation was in Carmel, located just a few blocks from the mission. My mom had apparently attended mass there years ago. My father had always told me that my mom loved this mission, so I made a point to walk over and visit it. As I entered the grounds, I was thrown off guard by a sudden feeling of sadness. It was as if it had possessed me. I sat down on a bench and openly wept, not caring that others were around. As grief cascaded over me like a waterfall, I realized that I had been at this very same church with my mother *in utero*. I had been there while inside her body.

When my sobs finally subsided, I looked up. It was a beautiful spring day. The sun was out, and the sky was a brilliant blue. Flowers were blooming and butterflies fluttering in the garden. As I turned my face toward the warmth of the sun, I felt a gentle breeze caress me. And then I realized that my mom and I were sitting together once more. In that moment, I felt profoundly loved.

There is a scripture verse, Revelation 21:4, that had always sounded like a fairy tale to me until that moment. I certainly didn't believe in it. It reads, "He will wipe every tear from their eyes. There will be no more death or mourning or crying or pain, for the old order of things has passed away."

Although I was crying in that moment, I was not in pain in the ways I had known before. I was experiencing a sense of deep relief that comes when only love abounds. I don't know why it took my mom's death to restore my sense of connection with her. I just know that the years the locusts had eaten were being restored.

Chapter 24

Take the Dance

I first tried surfing on a whim- catalyzed by a friend talking incessantly about it. It felt like those days in high school when everyone talked about sex and I didn't have a clue. I watched little kids on the beach, outfitted in wetsuits and learning how to pop up on the sand, and I thought, *If they can do, why can't I*? It was the kid in me watching that created a longing– a longing to play. Trapped in the isolation of adulthood, being single, and my own serious nature, I longed to do something fun!

Don't get me wrong; I'm not that girl who will jump off a cliff just because "everybody's doing it." But some impulses can't be explained. They're mysterious and spontaneous…and they change us.

True, I've had my moments of ridiculous impulses- like the time I put my foot in tar to see what the black ooze felt like, and the time I thought I could slide down a pole with no hands. The first incident resulted in hours of scrubbing my feet with turpentine; the other in a trip to the hospital. Both occurred when I was five. But at forty, I rarely did things on impulse. Burdened by years of grief and loss, I was one for hesitation versus risk.

In the film *Shall We Dance?* (the original Japanese version, not the remake with Richard Gere and Jennifer Lopez) a Japanese businessman mired in the monotony of corporate life stumbles across a ballroom dance studio and signs up for dance lessons on a whim. He does this in secret, because at the time in which the film is set, partnered dancing is considered taboo in Japan. We, the audience, then watch how the miracle of dance restores his suffocated soul. We see dance breathing life into him again.

All of us need passions in our lives, particularly during the hard work of transformation. In fact, it is passion and taking risks that often catalyzes transformation. When we've been pummeled by life circumstances and feel lost or dead inside, we need to feel life force moving through us.

Sadly, challenging events can seem to obliterate our passions. Even though our passions are lifelines, we can become so disconnected from them that we might not have the time, energy, motivation, or focus to pursue activities that we know would imbue our lives with meaning. Feeling consumed with worry or overburdened with tasks doesn't lend itself to *joie de vivre.*

Even when nothing traumatic has happened, the day-to-day responsibilities of adulthood can abort our pursuits to live a passionate and meaningful life. It was hard for me to commit to being a theatre major in college, even though acting and writing were my passions. Majoring in theatre seemed frivolous compared to a degree in biology or political science. I felt that if I studied theatre I wasn't being responsible, because it was fun. It was hard work, yet it made me so happy. It was unfamiliar to equate discipline with such fantastic joy!

I wish someone had told me how important it is to follow one's passions. I ended up sticking with the theatre major, but I still refused to see my studies as a legitimate path. Ultimately, in not fully committing to the career I wanted, I blocked a fundamental aspect of my being.

This morning I had chores to do, bills to pay, and emails to answer, plus I needed to work on this book. But at 9:45, I jumped in the car and drove to the YMCA for my ten o'clock Bollywood dance class. I knew I was going to be late- but even forty-five minutes of dance (as opposed to an hour) was better than none at all.

It was inconvenient to stop what I was doing so that I could dart off to the class. I didn't like being rushed and feeling scattered. However, as soon as I put on my hip scarf and felt the coins across my waist jingle, I smiled- and within ten minutes, I saw that the woman looking back at me from the mirror was laughing and smiling, and that despite being forty-seven, her face was that of a radiant young girl.

Dance, clearly, is another passion of mine. It reminds me of my identity as a performing artist. It validates who I am as an actor and dancer. It also informs me that I need creativity like I need oxygen. Writing isn't enough. I need performing arts too.

Life itself is a dance we can engage with or observe. We can stand on the sidelines watching wistfully, but we can also make other choices. If someone asks us to dance, for example, do we say yes? And if no one asks, do we have the courage to step out on the floor anyway?

In life, opportunities cross our path and we have to decide whether to take them or let them pass. Do we let ourselves fall in love? Take that trip? Quit our job? Try something new? How do we know when to dance and when to sit it out?

Recently I was cogitating about a decision to do something that was a bit on the bold side and involved some risk. I spoke to a friend about it- he's in his seventies- and after listening to me he quietly said, "It's not my place to tell you what to do. Yet I invite you to consider the dance, because when you get to be my age, the dance comes around less frequently." I will never forget him saying that to me. When we realize how precious and short life is, we begin to embrace it more fully and more urgently.

After my mom died I was lucky to find a sense of rejuvenation in surfing. I took up the sport the same year as her death. In a way this is lovely and symbolic, as my mom and I took many trips to the beach together. Perhaps those memories were part of the allure.

As I wrote in an earlier chapter, surfing is incredibly spiritual. When you catch a wave, you are in tandem with a moving force of nature. You become one with the wave- and afterwards, I can feel the movement of the wave within me, even hours later. It is as if the sea is still rocking me with its undulations. I feel the ocean as a body memory that permeates the cells of my being. If that is not God, I don't know what is.

Chapter 25

Just Breathe Through It

Many of us have been in a yoga or exercise class where the teacher serenely says, "Just breathe through it," while we're swearing beneath our breath because we're holding some ridiculous position or are doing an endless number of crunches that make our stomachs burn as if they're on fire. "I don't *want* to breathe through it!" we often scream in our heads. "I just want this pain to stop!"

What do our teachers mean when they say, "Just breathe through it" like a bleeping mantra? What is breath and why is it so powerful?

While breathing seems simple, it's actually something we resist doing when we are scared or in pain. We'd rather not "breathe through it." We'd prefer to avoid it– whatever "it" is– and breathing makes us feel it.

The truth, of course, is that the feeling is there whether we surrender to it or not. We're deluding ourselves when we think we can bypass pain by holding our breath. In fact, pain magnifies when we try to suppress it. Like a damned-up river, once our floodgates open, the feelings will flow forth in full force.

We don't really have to do anything to "breathe through it," because all of us are breathing. We do it naturally. If we weren't breathing, we'd be dead. But if we invite the breath in more consciously and more fully, we ease the process considerably.

The more we restrict the natural flow of oxygen moving through us, in contrast, the more we deny ourselves valuable nourishment. This is unfortunate, as it starts to inhibit transformation on the biological level. When we don't breathe, our bodies do not get the full replenishment they need for optimal functioning.

Restricting the breath also inhibits transformation on the psycho-spiritual level, because it impedes our emotional experience. We need the breath to help transmute raw emotion in a natural, organic way that leads to eventual release. Otherwise, we're in danger of discharging emotions in destructive, unpredictable ways.

Why is a woman in labor told to breathe, breathe, and breathe? Because she's pushing to bring new life into being.

When she holds her breath, she makes things more difficult for herself and the labor. When she breathes, she can push more easily. When we breathe in and out, we too are bringing new life to our experience.

When we "breathe through it," we can feel the breath's power to cleanse, sustain, and revitalize every aspect of our being. In fact, the word breath in Hebrew (*ruach*), in Greek (*pneuma*) and Sanskrit (*prana*) are synonymous with the words "spirit" or "wind." This indicates a link between our breath, being, and the divine. Our breath is the life force that helps us fully embrace and enjoy the moment. It is also a conduit for transformation.

All of this sounds nice, but when we're going through excruciating times, we're like the pregnant woman who wants to say to everyone around her telling her to breathe to "f--- off!" Transformation is brutal work, and sometimes the labor is so long and torturous it feels like we'll die. How do we breathe through the pain of rape, violence, illness, betrayal, or injustice? It's hard to go all yoga-Zen in these moments. How do we endure?

One of the most beautiful passages ever written on transformation- often called "The Valley of the Dry Bones"- specifically refers to the breath. It also refers to profound violence and a need to transcend it. The passage is in the biblical book of Ezekiel and the idea is that through the Spirit and through breath, even dry bones can live again. We can have restoration and healing.

The book Ezekiel focuses on fundamental questions we are still asking today: How do traumatized people restore their hearts and souls? How do humans find meaning, hope, and life after profound brutality? How do cultures that have been decimated, exterminated or marginalized ever experience wholeness again? How do survivors survive? How can we face the horrors of man's inhumanity to man and not have our hearts turn to stone? How do people receive new hearts?

These are the challenges of healing trauma on personal and political levels. This is the work of transformation. And as trite as it may sound, part of the answer to these questions lies in "breathing through it." Miraculously, through inhalation and exhalation, we breathe new life into every fundamental level of existence.

There is also a practical level to consider when reflecting on the notion of "breathing through it." We need to actually breathe versus intellectually reflect on breathing. We want to make the process of breathing as simple as possible. We don't have to engage in fancy, complicated breathing exercises. We can simply imagine our breath coming in and out like an ocean wave - back and forth, back and forth. I also find it helpful to lift my arms on the inhalation and to drop them on the exhalation. This gives a very simple action to coordinate with my breath. While we do this, we have only to observe the thoughts, feelings, and sensations that arise while we're breathing. There is nothing to control, fix, stop, or judge. There is nothing we have to "do." We can just be.

I find ocean waves have a wonderful correlation with breath. Staring at the waves reminds me of this. Initially just subtle movements on the horizon, they slowly build. Sometimes they peter out, dissipating almost to stillness- but not quite. When barely perceptible to the eye, waves stay in motion, like a quiet, persistent heartbeat. They are a constant inhalation and exhalation. They are steady in energetic transformation. They crash to the shore, recede, and then begin the cycle all over again.

Perhaps this is the *ruach*, the *pneuma*, and the *prana* that great traditions have referred to over the centuries and that assist with transformation. Perhaps calling on this force is how we "just breathe through it."

Chapter 26

Death in Transformation

"Weird and uncomfortable are invitations; pain is a signal," my yoga teacher said one evening in class. We were lying on our backs with blocks positioned under our rib cages and necks. This left the heart cavity rather open and exposed.

We moderns have a tendency to hold the exact opposite posture. Sitting at desks hunched over our computers, we often collapse our chests into concave positions. Furthermore, many of us unconsciously guard our hearts by wrapping our arms around our bodies self-consciously.

When we do something new it often feels weird. We can interpret that strangeness as an error. But my teacher was suggesting that it can mean something entirely different. While pain is always a signal that something is wrong (and that we

142

should stop doing whatever is inflicting it), "different" or "uncomfortable" often leads to something better.

All learning requires discombobulation. A schoolteacher of mine once said, "Confusion is a sign of learning." My little mind thought this was a complete contradiction. How could learning be confusing? It was supposed to be clarifying. But as an adult, I've learned that's not always the case. On the road to mastery, we scramble our preexisting knowledge base. We stretch our minds outside of their comfort zones. I studied Greek years ago and I recall saying many times in frustration, "This is Greek to me!"

Then, suddenly, Greek *was* Greek to me. I could read it. The hieroglyphics made sense.

Why, then, do we resist the weird and uncomfortable? These things could be portals to the unknown, leading to something affirmative and good- so what are we afraid of?

When we break patterns we become disoriented. What was once engrained and regular gets deconstructed and then reintegrated into a new form. This is the essence of transformation. It demands that we break outdated modes of being.

Weird and uncomfortable are not necessarily hard to deal with when the changes are subtle and slight. When we experience RADICAL transformation, however, we can actually feel as if we're dying. And this becomes one of the most challenging aspects to manage when healing from profound wounds. When in the heart of transformation, we can experience an enormous amount of intra-psychic chaos and uncertainty. Our inability to tolerate such states can lead to negative coping strategies, such as dependence on drugs and alcohol, unhealthy relationship patterns, and venting our emotions in unhealthy ways.

On a metaphoric level, one might refer to such a condition as a *bardo* state. *Bardo* is a Tibetan word that means a transition or gap between one situation and the beginning of another. Tibetans use the word to describe the intermediate stage between death and rebirth but it also has a broader, more complex meaning. By definition, the word crystallizes the process of transition itself- and its resulting chaos. While terrifying, this period of suspension between one form and another describes the process of transformation itself, in which the old must give way for the new.

When interfacing with my mother's alcoholism, most of my experience in childhood and adolescence could be described as a *bardo* state. I felt everything had an aspect of uncertainty. Would she drink, or would she not? Were things going to get better or worse?

When her depression intensified and she became suicidal, I found myself living in a constant, and even more pronounced, state of the unknown.

When the floodgates of emotion open we can experience an overwhelming sense of free fall that overwhelms us. In the heart of profound suffering we can feel as if we're having a break*down* instead of a break*through*. The intensity of our feelings can create a sensation of psychic disintegration; we feel as if we're dying. But we're not. On the contrary, we are in the process of being reborn. If we can hang on, our pain becomes transmuted and integrated, creating the spaciousness within our psyche necessary for something else to emerge.

In nature, the process of transformation is one in which living things die and then reemerge. A flower blooms, its petals wither and fall to the ground, and then its seeds give birth once again. Yet this process of constant change, so natural and organic, is something that humans resist because it doesn't always feel good. We resist change, trying to hold onto the old, not realizing that the more we fight these inevitable forces the more our suffering will increase. When we fail to understand this, we lose tremendous opportunities for growth.

Transformation coupled with profound suffering, then creates a crucible in which old aspects of the self deconstruct so that new dimensions and possibilities can arise. In the process, though, we might feel as if we have fallen into an existential pit of pain with no way out. If we find ourselves in this situation, it is important to remember that, as Victor Frankel once said, "What is to give light must endure burning."

In other words, sometimes the only way out of suffering is through it. In the process, we change alchemically, and ultimately separate the gold from the dross.

We Are Not Our Stories

One of the scariest moments in the transformation process is when we start to let go of our identification with our stories and traumas. We can absolutely experience the *bardo* state when we open to a new phase of our lives that is drastically different from the memories and events that once held center stage.

Remembering our stories of trauma matters. It's important to communicate and unburden them. It's important to share and to be witnessed. In fact, the primary solace of narration often comes from having an audience. When there are others around us, listening to our stories, we no longer are fully alone in our memories of experiences that caused us pain.

Retelling a story over and over, however, can reinforce it, thereby keeping us from transformation.

It's a fine line. Some feel adamantly that we should share until we no longer need to. It's no one's business to tell us when we should be done. And it's certainly no one's business to tell us what we do or don't feel, because our stories are etched into the landscapes of our psyches. No matter what anyone else says, those traces remain.

Freud wrote of "repetition compulsion"- a condition where people keep enacting aspects of their trauma with the hopes of mastering it, but they rarely succeed in doing so. This can certainly happen, but different results are also possible. In play therapy with children, for example, repetition compulsion usually gives way to new narratives. Kids eventually get bored with the old "play" and create something new.

Is it possible to start identifying with a narrative to the point that it defines our lives and limits possibilities? Is it easier to keep telling the same old story because it's familiar and has become our identity? Do we do this because it's too terrifying to face the blank page and not know what the story is? What if the new story is boring? What if there's nothing juicy or dramatic about it?

Letting go of the story can be excruciating. It can lead to moments of feeling sheer nothingness. Emptiness. The void. It can even mimic serious depression- but it's not depression. It's transformation.

What helps is remembering that we get to be the authors of our lives. We get to create the story's end. While there may be a blank page, we hold the pen. There needs to be a story arc and we get full creative license to shape it. We get to decide where our plot is headed. Unlike with those old stories we've been telling, we have so much more power and control than we realize. By deconstructing our narratives, we move into the imaginary realm and transcend ourselves. We get to become.

It's essential to remember that we are *not* our stories. We are not even the characters we play in those stories. These are all just aspects of ourselves- and that is why people so readily relate to what we tell them. They see parts of their own experiences in our narratives. Our stories hold pieces of their stories.

When we see that our stories are part of us but not all of us, we make room for new stories to emerge. This is how we continually lean into transformation. But parts of us have to keep dying and rejuvenating in the process.

Chapter 27

Wrestling With Waiting

Most of us have done a fair amount of waiting. It's a part of life. Yet there are times when waiting starts to feel like we're living in a bad production of *Waiting For Godot*.

There are so many ways in which we wait. "Your time will come," people will say while we wait for a job, meal, paycheck, or diagnosis. We wait for good or bad news, for the traffic to lift, for the storm to clear, or for that lucky break; we wait for others to change; we wait for love to finally arrive.

In today's instant-gratification culture, waiting has become harder. We can no longer tolerate standing in line at a store without checking our phones or making calls. When we arrive at the counter, we nod to that checker as if he or she was a mere servant inconveniencing us and then we promptly ignore him or her.

If we're to undergo transformation, we need to become more comfortable with waiting and "dead" time. Because change is not instantaneous. It requires patience.

How, then, do we wait, and is there any benefit in the process? Is there a way out of existential angst, or are we relegated to it like it's purgatory? Can we resort to sex, drugs, or alcohol as an escape, or must we chin up like a little tin soldier? Do we collapse and fall apart or scale the mountain to greatness?

Again, this is where being mindful of our breathing can help. Our breath is our life force and it helps us move through each moment. In yoga, for example, the space between the breaths is viewed as a transition point. The point where inhalation gives way to exhalation and then gives rise to inhalation again is considered the movement of life.

It's not fun to feel painful emotions, but it is this arc that gives rise to desire, momentum, action, and transformation. It seems we are endlessly waiting with nothing happening, and yet underneath the surface, progress occurs. Micro-movements yield to bigger ones, just like in time-lapse photography. What feels like a boring time might actually be a highly creative one. A little physical movement can remind us that movement is occurring on deeper levels as well.

When we're at an impasse in our lives, it can be frustrating. The times when things are fun, exciting and sexy are much more desirable and pleasurable. I often think of the Olympic athletes. We see them at the height of their game. We celebrate with them when they perform amazing feats and shine in full glory standing on the podium. Yet beneath those scenes are endless periods of waiting and tedium. The swimmer who had to be in the pool at 5:00 a.m. every morning and the skater who had to be on the ice each day *no matter what* know about waiting. Champions are not made overnight. It takes years before they can harvest their hard work.

The hardest periods of waiting, though, are those that we go through with no goal in sight. When we have no hope. When we feel lost and don't know if there is any way out of the labyrinth. Waiting, when it seems we have nothing to wait for except a terrible void can become excruciating and depressing.

My own worst period of waiting was the seven days in between receiving a suicide note from my mom and the news that she was dead: July 11th to July 18th, 2008. During that week, as I waited for news whether she was dead or alive, I had to figure out what to do with myself. State surveyors who inspect hospitals for standards and accreditation were at the facility where I worked that week, so I had to be there. I wasn't allowed to take time off. In fact, I was told that unless my mother was indeed dead, I had to be at work. I couldn't believe the callousness of my employers: we were an organization dealing with mental health, yet no one was concerned about my own. Going into work proved to be a good use of my time, however. It allowed me to focus on other people and things, and to put one foot in front of the other.

For a few days I went through the motions, compartmentalizing. I glided along the pond like a duck; underneath I was paddling like hell. After work, I swam, my senses and memories heightened as I propelled my body through the water. The pool sometimes felt like a large amniotic sac. And as I walked out to the parking lot with wet hair, I couldn't help but notice the mothers and daughters around me. I thought of how my mother used to pick me up from various places: Girl Scouts, catechism, school, and day care. I remember holding her hand as we crossed parking lots, me traipsing along besides her, telling her about my day and what I wanted for dinner. I remembered being close to my mom, sitting on the couch as she read aloud to me and I studied the words on the page, unconsciously teaching myself to read.

At home, to feel close to her again and to pass the time, I read Nancy Drew books, which both my mother and I had always loved.

Just when I'd begun to believe my mom was alive, the call came late Friday morning. Almost a week had passed with no news, and I'd started to breathe easier. And then, I heard an unfamiliar man's voice over the phone.

"Is this Lise Porter?" he asked.

I'd gotten calls like this before. A hospital nurse or doctor informing me that my mom was in the ER. I waited, half expecting to hear the news that, yes, she was still alive but was in a hospital somewhere. But the man didn't follow the script. Instead, he informed me that she was dead.

She'd been alive up until the previous night. Shopkeepers had seen her milling about in front of their stores the day before. They thought she was homeless.

She was found dead on the street, in front of the stores. The police reassured me there had been no foul play. Pills were scattered around her, and a few were in a little plastic bag with her booking number on it. She died from acute intoxication of amitriptyline, a medication given for sleep and to calm nerves. The jail had apparently released her with the pills.

The kind of waiting that ends in great tragedy can bring a sense of death to our spirits. But in death there is always transformation.

One of the reasons I'm such a fan of creativity is that it enables us to find shards of meaning in the rubble of our lives. As we pick up the pieces and place them here and there, we start to form a mosaic of healing.

Learning how to sit through the transitions of felt sensate experience without repressing or collapsing is a challenge. It can be its own Gethsemane. We often suffer alone while the disciples sleep. Yet we die and are reborn in each impasse if we allow ourselves to breathe through it. It is the road to Spirit and to Grace.

CHAPTER 28

The Beauty of the Wolf

When I was a child, if I expressed anger, I was promptly told I was acting like a "little animal." I was to go to my room until I could act like a "little girl." Crying was allowed but the common temper fits of toddlerhood were unacceptable.

Years later, I struggled to register the emotion of anger. It took acting classes to access that feeling within me.

We live in a culture that is emotionally illiterate. At extremes, we numb everything out- through sex, food, substances, work, the Internet, and more- or we have meltdowns in the most inappropriate, unhealthy fashions. (At the most dangerous end of the spectrum, people lose their tempers while brandishing firearms).

All emotions- even ones we consider inappropriate- serve an evolutionary function. They tell us that something is wrong and that we need to respond to whatever is not right in the environment or our lives. Something needs attention. If we listen to our emotions, they provide us with invaluable clues and resources for our well-being: they tell us something needs to change. Without that insight, we would take no action. There would be no impetus for leaning in.

Anger in particular is a powerful force. I liken it to the quality of fire. When channeled appropriately, anger can change our lives for the better. It can liberate the world from injustice: like fire, it can bring warmth. But when not dealt with adequately, or not dealt with at all, it can be like a flame in a forest: it eventually consumes everything in its path.

Positive Uses of Anger

I find it disconcerting that when we're conditioned to "be nice," we often lose touch with the healthy dimensions of anger. Anger is a reaction to a real or perceived threat. It helps us set healthy boundaries, stand up to betrayals, and make positive changes in our lives. And yet so often, we are deemed rude, unreasonable, or bitchy when we express discontent, even if our feelings are completely justified. This is particularly true for women but applies to men too. All too often, we apologize for our feelings just after we've stood up for ourselves. We get served up a plate of manure and say, "Thank you, thank you very much," instead of saying, "No thanks. That is crap."

I think of the wonderful film *Wolf*, with Jack Nicholson and Michelle Pfeiffer. Nicholson's character, Will, has been grossly taken advantage of by a colleague at work: the guy not only steals his job, but also sleeps with his wife. Resentful but passive, Will swallows his fate- until one night he is bitten by a wolf, and the spirit of the animal enters him. Suddenly, his instincts are fully alive. He is no longer a tame, domesticated drone who doesn't know how to fend for his dignity or life. Instead he takes his power back in beautiful ways.

I think of my beloved cat, Hafiz, who used to always hiss at the vet. At home, Hafiz was docile and loving, but when he felt threatened, he knew how to protect himself.

Would a mother wolf teach her cubs to let predators harm them? Absolutely not! So why do we let people hurt us, smiling as if it is no big deal when we've been wronged? Why are we afraid of hurting the feelings of the people who have shamelessly hurt us?

The animal within us all is that part of us that recognizes danger, recognizes bullshit, even when it's disguised as filet mignon. It also recognizes when we're safe and protected, and when we are being treated with respect. The spirit of the wolf is a beautiful thing. We can all learn from it.

The Taste of Bitter

The flip side of transformative anger is the kind that keeps us stuck in bitterness for years. This kind of anger can be lethal and is completely counter to growth and change.

Most people have heard the cliché that not forgiving is like drinking poison. The anger and frustration we feel about a situation can turn to venom within our bodies, threatening to destroy us. We want the person who harmed us to suffer, but in the end we are the ones damaged by not forgiving. And sometimes it's not a person we're angry at but life itself.

I remember reflecting on this when teaching a psychology class at a local community college. The course contained a section on relationships and romantic love. One night, as conversation ensued, an older female student piped up with, "All that princess bullshit. It's garbage! I've never seen a happy marriage. I never got my happily ever after, and I've never known anyone who did either. It's all bullshit!"

The class suddenly became very quiet, and I found myself struck by the pain behind that student's words. I could tell that underneath her rage, deep sadness and disappointment lurked, and so did a profound longing for love. But her anger and bitterness were so fierce they were bound to drive any person who might offer her that love away- reaffirming her belief that "love was bullshit." Without healing, her inability to forgive had the potential to become a self-fulfilling prophecy, so that she missed out on love and became bitter, or at least up until that point.

Bitterness can swallow us whole: that is its danger. The feeling can completely consume us, threatening to drain our vitality- and not only that, it carries a stench somewhat like a skunk's. When we reek of bitterness, other people can smell it, and they try to get as far away from us as possible.

But there is also danger in attempting to bypass the challenging feelings we experience. Like an abscess that needs to drain, we have to embrace bitterness for a time, giving it a voice and letting it express its power and righteous indignation. If we don't, we lose the opportunity to let that bitterness soften to grief. When our tears finally fall, they wash out the wounds lodged in our hearts.

I once participated in a psychodrama workshop that explored themes from *The Wizard of Oz*. In one of the exercises, I was asked to step into the role of the bad witch, which I welcomed, because I had played Dorothy in a childhood production. As Dorothy and her little friends came prancing down the yellow brick road, I stepped onto a chair and hovered above them. "Hello, my pretty!" I cackled in a high-pitched voice.

Initially, I loved the thrill of power I felt as they all cowered in my presence. But as I continued with my bullying tirade, I began to feel lonely. As I improvised, I was shocked at how much rage I felt— at Dorothy for having friends and support, at their happiness and camaraderie, and by what I perceived constituted their happy lives. Suddenly, real tears were smarting in my eyes for all the ways in which I identified with the witch. Even though on the surface I was Dorothy— a friendly, likeable person with a good life— on the inside there were so many deep wounds no one saw or knew about that I understood the rage and isolation of the witch. If I wasn't careful, I could easily become her. If anything ripped down the walls I had constructed to protect my heart from where it had been bludgeoned, a raging animal would be set loose.

When We Displace Our Anger

One of the things that can happen when we haven't worked through anger issues is that we can displace our negative emotions onto the wrong people. Our anger can leak out, leading us to attack people who have little or nothing to do with our misfortunes.

We can also take out our frustrations on people who seem to have things easier than we do. When we feel hurt and disappointed, we can look at others who seem to be thriving (and lucky) and lash out at them. For instance, I know someone whose grandson told a schoolmate he was going to Disneyland for his birthday. The other little boy, distressed and jealous that he wasn't going to the "happiest place on earth," punched my friend's grandson in the face.

Even if we never say or do anything outwardly angry, our bitter thoughts and energy often reflect the resentment that comes with an inability to forgive. Sometimes we aren't angry at specific people but we may still feel bitter, perhaps at the world at large or at God. I witnessed this years ago when I worked with emotionally disturbed children, and saw how they would pick up chairs and throw them, bite peers, or bang their own heads against the wall in emotional frustration.

Because anger is so explosive, we have to learn constructive ways of dealing with it. One the other hand, because it is such an informative and powerful healing agent, we never want to eradicate it altogether. Owning our lives entails learning how to capture anger and use it for our own benefit. Then we find the hardness in our hearts melting like butter on pancakes- and suddenly, life is much more satisfying.

Chapter 29

Tribe is a Myth

It is absolutely essential that we have love and community in our lives, yet a huge stumbling block to transformation is believing we need a special tribe to encourage us. Do we need a select group of people who share all our values and who are similar to us? I question the myth that in order to flourish we need a large following of people who "get" us and love us unconditionally.

In some ways this belief is similar to the one that if we find the right romantic partner, we will live happily ever after. While it's true that being loved unconditionally by a select group of people and by a partner are amazing gifts and blessings, transformation isn't contingent on it. Nor is an inclusive, supportive community immune from dysfunction. Human beings are fundamentally flawed, so relying on a "tribe" to complete us is a setup for disillusionment and disappointment. At some point our "tribe" will disappoint us or disapprove of what we're doing. They may even kick us out or scapegoat us.

Deep and profound transformation requires an enormous amount of courage. It demands that we have the ability to stand in our truths even when others don't support or understand us. That is why the notion of tribe is a myth. Strong, successful individuals and leaders often stand alone even when amongst others.

When we undergo transformation the resulting changes can be inherently threatening to a group. If anything, we may lose our tribe. Relationships can realign, fracture, or split. We may have long stretches of being alone, and we may have a whole new set of people come into our lives.

As a single person with no children and with deceased parents, the notion of a "tribe" is somewhat alien to me. Perhaps pining after this supposed tribe can keep us trapped from evolving and embracing our lives. When I've spent considerable time disappointed about not having a big, happy clan surrounding me, I've actually negated other people and experiences of value. Not only that, at the end of the day, we determine our destiny and our happiness. No one can do that for us, even if we have an entire cheerleading team rooting for us.

It may be that the concept of tribe is more akin to a patchwork quilt. We have different people in our lives that bring richness to it. No one person or entity completes the quilt. Instead the quilt is comprised of many different relationships from all walks of life.

In the fifteen years that I lived in San Diego I had a kaleidoscope of connections. There were wonderful friendships with my neighbors. There was the family that hosted an annual pumpkin carving block party, and my landlord, who lived in the house in front of me and became like a cherished father and friend. I was close with his daughters as well, even more so after their dad died suddenly of leukemia. I had people I adored at my church and colleagues scattered across the country that I taught with, sharing laughter, tears, and glasses of wine in various restaurants across the nation. My cats, Rumi and Hafiz, snuggled with me every morning, noon, and night.

Now that I'm living in Los Angeles I'm creating a new web of people who enrich my life as I do theirs. These connections are at times fleeting and not yet cemented. Instead they are more like beads being strung on a necklace strand. It begins with a conversation here, a conversation there, or a wave at a neighbor that eventually leads to breaking bread. It occurs when I stand in a circle at my Bollywood dance class each week and extend my arms as if giving flowers to the same women, young and old, and we laugh and gyrate our hips together while the coins on our hip scarves shimmer and make joyous sounds. It happens when I meet other film artists every few weeks to discuss upcoming projects, hopes and dreams.

Without a doubt meaningful relationships and community are important. We need, however, to expand our view of who comprises our social networks.

We're living through a period in our nation's history, though, where clinging to the notion of tribe could be our demise. Intolerance promotes dissension. Refusing to acknowledge or respect our fellow citizens because they are different from us divides humanity. Being so caught up on our notion of tribe that we only fraternize with people of our own age, race, class, marital status, or religion creates a narrow-minded life. It generates a climate in which marginalizing others becomes the norm. Then we no longer have the United States of America. We have the United States of Ourselves. And a house divided by factions cannot stand.

While transformation may set us apart from people we once thought were "in our camp," it also reveals to us that this notion of solidarity can be a mirage in the desert- one that is ultimately destructive. When we deeply transform our lives, we become more unified with ourselves. This in turn helps us establish more pure and authentic relationships with others. When we feel right with ourselves, we are more available and loving to others. That is a better basis for tribe than sharing the same political views or liking the same television shows.

When we rely too much on the tribe for respect and approval, we forget that all of us are struggling. Most of us are so caught up in our own "stuff" that we're not even thinking of others. We're in such a self-absorbed state that we don't have the time or energy to hold others up or tear them down. Instead we're obsessing about ourselves. It's best not to look to the peanut galleries to define us.

Recently I was teaching a class on mental health that dealt with adolescent development and wellness. A discussion about social media ensued, as it is such a prominent aspect of teenagers' lives today. I was deeply struck by a comment someone made about Facebook. "It's like, 'I post, therefore I am,'" the individual remarked, indicating that some teens are so desperate for approval from their peers on social media that they don't feel the importance of their existence without it.

This made me very sad. Our sense of identity should not be based on how many "likes" we get on FB when we post a photo or make a comment: it should stem from a deep well within. It can then be reinforced by the validation we give ourselves, and the validation we receive from a few select and trusted people.

This is tribe redefined. And that is enough: it is more than enough. It is a tremendous treasure.

CHAPTER 30

Will You Play With Me?

The other day within an hour of being around a family friend's child, the little boy approached me and with quiet earnestness asked, "Will you play with me?" When I nodded yes, he gently led me to the living room where his toys were scattered, and we began to play.

Although the toys were appealing, what fascinated the little boy most was the switch that could dim the lights. As he lowered the lights, making the room grow dark he pronounced, "Now it is night." Taking my cue, I rolled over on my side and began to gently snore. Then the lights came back up. "Now it's day." I stretched out my arms and sighed, opened my eyes and said, "Good morning." Looking at him I continued, "I'm hungry. Are you hungry? What shall we have for breakfast?"

We settled on pancakes and bacon and then went through the procedure again. The lights dimmed, I snored, the lights came back up, I awakened and then we ate pancakes. We did this at least ten times validating that Freud's theory of repetition compulsion is most definitely an aspect of children's play and a mechanism through which they can explore the events they observe on a daily basis.

It never fails to amaze me how much children both yearn and need to play. It is not to be underestimated. The therapeutic benefits of play are profound, which is why some of us psychotherapists use it as a central part of our work. But it isn't just children who need to play. We all do. Animals. Children. Adults. All of us benefit from the intimate contact that comes through play as we enter the portals of our imaginations with others. So in a way, those five innocent words– "Will you play with me?"- are like a secret password. If taken seriously, the words initiate us into a very specific form of delight, exploration, and experience of each other's company.

While all humans have a capacity for spontaneity and joy, life experiences often hinder the regularity of play in our lives. Trauma, in fact, can abort it. I look back at my childhood and see patterns where play simply stopped. I think of the adults who would routinely say, "Not now, honey. We'll play later." I also remember when my mom started drinking to the point of blacking out. Focusing on my mom's well-being became more important than slumber parties or playing dress-up.

As adults, many things interfere with our ability to play. We are told to grow up and get serious. There are bills to pay, chores to do, and problems to solve. In my life, these attitudes were passed on to me in my DNA- initially costing me an acting career (because to act for a living would be the height of frivolity, right?). For many of us, play is something that comes at the end of the to-do list and sometimes simply gets channeled into sex, the consummate form of adult recreation. We forget the deeper needs behind the simple phrase, "Will you play with me?"- and instead of inviting others in, we tune them out or tell them they aren't playing right. We tell them to get off the playground or that they're not good enough for our team. Some of us break the rules and hurt others.

True play invites personal transformation. It creates an environment of exploration and curiosity. Because it involves the imagination, new possibilities emerge- initially as a template of fantasy, but with the power to become reality. Real change in our life occurs when we wed imagination with constructive action.

Part of owning our lives involves making space for play. What do we enjoy doing that invokes a childlike lightheartedness and what stimulates the imagination? Whatever activities we choose, creativity helps us organize the chaos of our lives. It is the opposite of destruction. In an age where tensions are rising and impulse control is diminishing, we need tools that preserve life rather than destroy it. When stress pushes us to the breaking point, we need a different type of weapon.

Play comes into our lives when we invite in the energy of the Divine; when we look at the ocean and see the way it dances. Play comes when we can relinquish worry and reclaim deeper pieces of ourselves. It is, in fact, a serious matter. It is how we master life.

Play also informs us of when we are in transition and when it's time for something new. Think about children playing the same scenario over and over again. They do this to master a concept or theme in their lives. Then they become bored and move on to a new game or skit. But they only abandon that first theme when they are ready to move on to the next one. Similarly, when we adults play at one scenario long enough to be bored with it, we too evolve and move on to something new and more reflective of where we're at in our lives.

How many of us have been playing out the same themes over and over again in our personal lives? Perhaps it's that same dysfunctional relationship pattern or taking the same unfulfilling jobs. When do we know it's time to try a new game with new players and new rules?

A degree of boredom also informs the process. If we're constantly entertained or overstimulated, there is no room for the idleness that often engenders daydreams, innovation, and clarity. Think of the lazy days of childhood, when time stretched before us seemingly endlessly. The boredom could be wearisome, yet it was good for us. I remember my toddler cousin once had nothing to play with in the car for two hours while we were on a drive somewhere, and he entertained himself with a straw for the entire ride. That straw was the best toy ever because he found multiple ways to be fascinated by it.

Whenever I have the rare afternoon where I don't have work to do or I'm not relaxing with a novel, I try to lean into the ensuing boredom and loneliness I might be feeling, because that is often when I get my best ideas for what to do next in my life. There are afternoons that I know I could fill with Amazon streaming or surfing the Internet or cleaning the house, but I stop myself and instead try to find ways to play. Should I draw or paint? Go for a walk in the hills? Is there a friend I can call to go out with? Should I strap my surfboard on my car and go splash in the sea? These activities, which we often dismiss as being "for children," are vital to our well-being. How can we maintain the elasticity and flexibility necessary to transformation if we don't ever exercise the muscles that were vital to us as children? Play increases our emotional flexibility, spontaneity, and adaptability.

In creativity and play, we want to have a degree of freedom and ease, yet at the same time take the risks that will allow us to excel and grow. Creativity demands that we walk along the edge of the unknown. It takes us into new places, which can scare and inhibit us, as well as delight us. We become like Dorothy- at first terrified and then thrilled to see life in Technicolor. As we journey through Oz, we find ourselves coming home to deeper truths once more, and are reminded that there is no place like home.

Chapter 31

Trusting Transformation

The other day, as I was pulling out of a gas station in Los Angeles, I noticed two women helping a blind young man learn to navigate on his own using a walking stick. They were walking slightly ahead of him and encouraging him forward with their voices. The older of the two women saw me in the car and signaled to the younger woman to have the boy wait—but the younger women shook her head vehemently and motioned for me to halt, which I was planning on doing anyway.

She wanted the boy to have courage and confidence. She wanted him to claim his path. Cars could wait for a blind pedestrian. He had the right to be dauntless.

Only cars don't always wait anymore. Not for blind people, or little old ladies crossing the street, or veterans in wheelchairs. The older woman knew this: the younger one did too. The difference between the two was that the younger woman wanted the boy to fully live his life despite the risks that entailed.

It's terrifying to walk straight into the unknown and not be able to see where we're going. It is a complete trust- an act of faith. Because of this, the blind boy and the two women took my breath away.

An hour later I was on the highway and found myself behind a truck. Written on the vehicle were the words, "Helping Hands for the Blind."

Okay. The universe isn't subtle. It hit me over the head with a two-by-four. Obviously, this was lesson I needed to grasp.

Do we have the faith of the blind? Can we walk with ease on paths we cannot see? And who will guide us as we step out? From where do we get our vision and courage?

There is no map or GPS navigation system for personal transformation. Instead, life asks us to journey completely into the unknown in order to achieve transformation. Of course, most of us fear the unknown, so we fear transformation. Part of the work, therefore, is to step out into our lives with more courage.

In acting class there is an exercise called a "frozen reading," in which two actors are given a scene they haven't set eyes on before and are instructed *not* to read it. Instead, they are told to look at each other. Only when they are locked onto each other's eyes can the person with the first line look down at the script. He or she is to read the line quickly, grab the words, and then deliver them while looking right back at his or her scene partner.

Basically, the exercise is a walk into the unknown. It feels kind of like walking off a cliff and not knowing where you'll land. The exercise makes me feel vulnerable because I don't know what is going to happen. And that is precisely the point of it. The exercise forces me to be fully in the moment and relational. If I'm looking at my partner I'm not thinking about how I'm going to deliver my next line. Instead I am completely connected to him or her, and I begin to respond to what is unfolding in real time: my partner smiles, my partner twitches, we burst into a nervous giggle, and a certain strange sexual chemistry unfolds even though the script doesn't indicate romance. Or, perhaps, the script's words are about love, yet my partner stares coldly at me and I in turn deliver my line in clipped tones....

This exercise is about letting go of preconceived notions and allowing the moment to unfold as it is meant to. For someone who likes to be in control (like me), this can be challenging. But it's a great rehearsal for life. Can I let go and see what happens? Can I be open to new experiences? Can I love? Can I perform without a safety net? Can I invite new possibilities in?

Great art emerges from risk-taking and generosity. Playing things safe does little for creation. The same holds true for life. Our best moments often stem from walking straight into the unknown. It's a form of acting on the edge, and it's essential to transformation.

In this state of not knowing, we can feel a degree of anxiety. One day I was talking with a friend about this.

"It's hard to break out of your comfort zone without orbiting into sheer panic," I said. "There has to be middle ground, right?"

"Oh, that's what our son's school calls the 'learning zone,'" my friend replied. "There's the comfort zone, where no learning takes place: the panic zone, where you're so freaked your mind is paralyzed: and then there's the learning zone, where you're just able to take in new skills and lessons."

In therapy there is a similar concept, referred to as "titrating the anxiety." This describes when an individual's anxiety begins to increase because he or she is on the brink of a breakthrough and growth. It is a process of adding an unknown element to a known one and seeing how the two ingredients settle. Yet the resulting degree of anxiety shouldn't be so intense that it creates terror or paralysis that serves no one.

This directly correlates to my friend's comments. The comfort zone, although cozy for a time, leads to a premature death. When people say they've worked hard and now want to coast through life or that because they're a certain age, there's nothing left to learn, I cringe. It's *never* too late to learn: there is always so much more to discover, enjoy, and do!

When we adopt these limiting attitudes, we start to shrink. Suddenly, driving a car becomes too scary; packing a suitcase seems like a monumental task; and moving to a new place feels like moving to another planet. This paradigm will lock us into rigidity and fear for the rest of our lives. It is the complete opposite of transformation. The learning zone, on the other hand, describes the edge where we stretch but don't hurt ourselves.

The panic zone, in contrast, is a place of too much, too soon. It's the equivalent of throwing a kid into the deep end of the swimming pool and saying, "Swim!" That child will most likely not be fond of swimming sports as an adult. The learning zone takes place in an environment of excitement and stability, not fear and chaos.

Curiosity is what motivates a child to learn. She learns to crawl and walk because there is an object, pet, or person in her proximity that she wants explore. She hasn't a clue what she is doing or where she is headed: she just keeps her eye on the prize.

When I saw that young blind boy I had just moved to Los Angeles and was terrified to be starting a brand-new life. That boy gave me strength and reminded me that we often don't know the details of our journey. We can only take one step, but when we venture out in faith we can walk on water. It's only when we look down that our doubt can sink us. We must learn to trust transformation.

Chapter 32

Life is a Gift - Use Accordingly

Most of us have played the White Elephant game at holiday parties. Everybody brings a cheap, nonsense gift. Once all the presents are opened, participants decide whether to keep the gift they were given or to steal someone else's gift. Rarely do we get want what we get. Something always looks better.

What happens when we don't get the life we want? Do we try to trade it for another one, or do we work to be satisfied with what we have? What happens when, try as we might to be grateful, we remain unhappy? Is this a sign of supreme entitlement, or of a mood state that is hard to mitigate? Or is it time to make a shift, if we are capable?

My friend's daughter recently had a baby. To celebrate this wonder, there were actually four baby showers. You can imagine the number of "likes" the baby photos attracted on Facebook when the baby actually arrived!

The baby's new life is a gift. But time can tear away at that gift. Just this morning I read about an African American man held at gunpoint by police officers as he came out of the Yale library. The man is a student at Yale, but the police assumed he was a wanted criminal because of the color of his skin. This is one of too many examples that can wear down our sense that life is an awesome present. Life can knock us down or point the barrel of a gun in our face when we're simply going about our business.

Injustice and despair are real and they can erode the soul's spirit. They urinate on the precious gift of life, leaving us enraged or weeping or numb.

It isn't just the dramatic tragedies that can threaten our sense of passion and purpose, either. Day-to-day concerns and struggles can eat away at our happiness as well.

Remember the little wonders of childhood? Getting excited when a mother brought in cupcakes for someone's birthday, or watching snow fall for the first time? When I think of life's hardships, I also think of its magic, for it is the wonder of life that is the true gift of this world. That's why we go ga-ga over babies and puppies.

New creatures are in awe of their surroundings, and witnessing that awe reminds us to be. Every time my neighbor's one-year-old child steps outside, she points at a bird or a flower with a huge grin on her face. Then her little voice squeaks with delight. It's magical to watch.

While we can't have a lobotomy to erase despair, we can work to repair the brokenness around us. I hear the birds sing as I write this and realize it is their voices that help make us whole.

What we experience as we age and move through our lives reminds me of what happens to driftwood before washing up on shore. We may be deeply weathered by rough experiences in the same way that wood is beaten up by waves and stones, but like the driftwood, our best path is to not resist. Driftwood allows itself to be smoothed out in the process, ever more refined. This is transformation. This is what we can all strive for.

I started this book sharing about my mother's alcoholism and eventual suicide, two life circumstances that shaped the first thirty-nine years of my life profoundly. My mother's life and death will remain a part of my internal and external landscape, influencing much of who I am as an individual. But the insights and healing I've experienced in the aftermath have forever changed me as well. I have earned the lines in my face, as well as the wisdom in my eyes. In pain, we are all initiates on a path that leads to compassion for others and for ourselves.

Years ago I worked in an orthodox Jewish nursing home situated on the banks of the Hudson. Beautiful trees graced the sprawling back lawn that led down to the river's edge. Some of the residents in the nursing home were Holocaust survivors. One woman had a numbered tattoo on her arm and would scream in Polish if anyone tried to stop her when she attempted to leave the unit. I was overwhelmed by my residents' experiences, knowing they had endured unimaginable traumas. Yet somehow, they had made it to America, married, raised children and lived meaningful lives.

Speaking with the nursing home rabbi one day about all of this, he pointed out the window to a magnificent tree.

"Lise, do you see that tree there?"

I nodded. It was a majestic tree that stood tall with dignity, providing both aesthetic pleasure and shade.

"Do you see where it was struck by lightning?" he asked.

I looked closer- and for the first time noticed that in the middle of the tree's trunk there was a gaping hole where it had been scorched to the quick. Yet it had kept growing, despite its wound. And until the rabbi pointed out burn marks, all I had noticed was its height, fullness, and beauty.

"Trauma is like that," he said. "We can move on with our lives."

That conversation reminded me that if we want to understand transformation, we can look to nature. That same riverbank we were looking at in the height of summer would grow stark and desolate a few months later, when snow and ice would transform the landscape to grey. In March and April, the cold would give way to warmer temperatures and bluer skies. Underneath the ground, new life would spring forth in the form of tulips, crocuses, and daffodils. Pink and white buds would dot the trees, and everything would become as green as the Emerald City. How different the riverbed looked during the various seasons!

I mentioned earlier how I was expected to do a fair amount of gardening as a child. I initially wanted to rebel against this, but instead found I enjoyed it. As I pulled dead leaves from shrubs and pruned and repotted plants, my mind quieted until the only sound I perceived was the rustle of the wind. I discovered that cutting back limbs gave birth to new buds, and pulling weeds at their stems allowed other plants to breathe. As I thrust my fingers into the earth, I could feel the pulse of creation echoing back my existence. And as the sun nourished the plants I tended, it also sustained me.

Spending hours in the garden, I began to perceive a type of wisdom inherent in creation. Although they were not spelled out for me, I discovered truths in what unfolded daily. Creation and the creative process itself seemed to reflect aspects of the Divine. I perceived these as expressions of God's love and a form of regenerative grace.

We all have the seeds of transformation within us. We can restore our lives from decay to beauty. But we must step into the garden to do that, and we must be willing to get our hands dirty in the process. While we may not know when things will begin to bloom and take form, we can know that they will. When we invest time, patience, consistency, and love into our inner lives, beauty emerges in our external ones.

ABOUT THE AUTHOR

Lise Porter grew up in Southern California and lives in Los Angeles. A licensed Marriage and Family Therapist and drama therapist, she has contributed extensively to the mental health field. As a national trainer for Mental Health First Aid, USA she has been intimately involved with bringing mental health awareness to the general public. She has been published twice in the *International Journal for the Arts in Psychotherapy* and has taught at Mira Costa College and Antioch University in Seattle. You can learn more about her at www.liseporter.com.

47716193R00122

Made in the USA
San Bernardino, CA
07 April 2017